PARIS

TRADITIONS

PARIS TRADITIONS

Watson-Guptill

Publishing Director: Laura Bamford
Executive Editor: Mike Evans
Editor: Humaira Husain
Production Controller: Joanna Walker
Picture Research: Liz Fowler

Creative Director: Keith Martin
Executive Art Editor: Geoff Borin

First published in 1999 by **Hamlyn**, an imprint of Octopus
Publishing Group Limited, 2-4 Heron Quays, Docklands,
London E14 4JP

First published in the United States in 1999 by **Watson-Guptill
Publications**, 1515 Broadway, New York, New York 10036

Copyright ©1999 Octopus Publishing Group Limited

Library of Congress Catalog Card Number: 99-62659

ISBN 0-8230-5409-8

Printed and bound in China

CONTRIBUTORS

1 CHARLOTTE KELLY A post graduate in art and architecture, works as a picture researcher at the Bridgeman Art Library and recently co-ordinated the establishment of their new Parisian office.

2 CATHERINE MARCANGELI Art historian and writer, spent 18 months in New York on a Fulbright Scholarship, currently lecturing at the Sorbonne University in Paris.

3 ELAINE DEED A well-known fashion writer based in London, has written for national UK magazines and newspapers, currently working as Fashion Features Editor on *Tatler*.

4 DIANA CRAIG A much-published author writing on varied subjects such as Bible stories, Pagan festivals and mythology, with a particular interest in history, art and travel.

5 JACKUM BROWN Both a food and travel writer, has written two cookbooks published by Hamlyn, travelled extensively and also written articles abroad.

6 PAUL ROLAND Freelance journalist and writer, regular contributor to various publications in UK, Europe, Japan and the US including the UK *Mail on Sunday*, *Classic CD* and *Which? Compact Disc*. Contributing Editor to *Jazz Singers*, published in the UK by Hamlyn.

7 BRIAN GRANVILLE An established sports writer, published in national sports magazines including *Shoot!* Has also written regularly for *The Guardian*.

8 STEPHANIE DRIVER American writer and editor, currently London based, has previously published travel guides including some on areas of France, and various articles on the theatre.

CONTENTS

ARCHITEC

Text: Charlotte Kelly

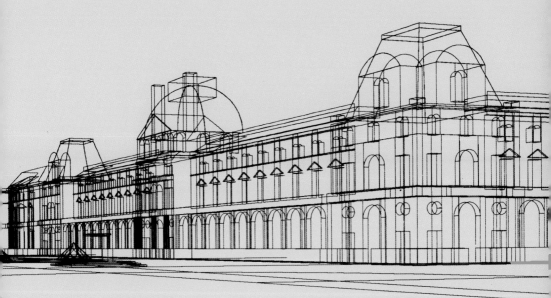

JRE

Paris has always celebrated itself through its grand architectural projects. A relatively recent one was the huge glass pyramid located in the courtyard of the Louvre which serves as an entrance to the museum.

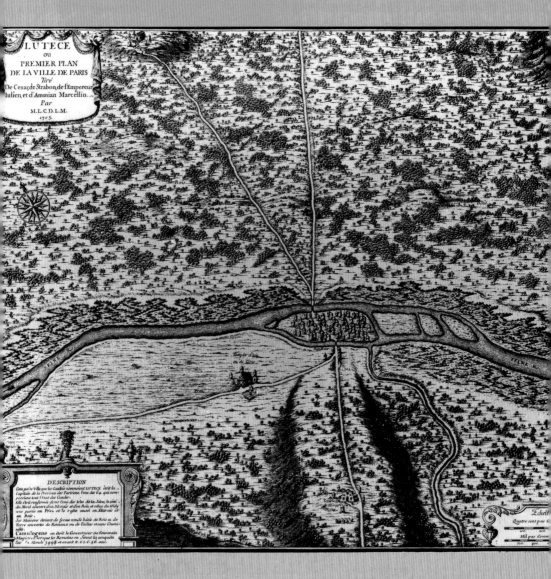

LUTECE
ou
PREMIER PLAN
DE LA VILLE DE PARIS
Tiré
De Cesar,de Strabon,de l'Empereur
Julien,et d'Ammian Marcellin.
Par
M.L.C.D.L.M.
1705.

DESCRIPTION

A s the cultural nexus of Europe, Paris has attracted some
of the best European architects, sculptors and masons
who have contributed to the creation of an eclectic
architectural legacy regarded by the French nation with civic
pride. The architectural beauty of Paris has also captured the
hearts of numerous visitors. The American writer Henry James
wrote of the city as 'Splendid, Paris most charming of cities',
Elizabeth Barrett Browning was similarly lavish in her praise,
'The city swims in verdure, beautiful as Venice on the waters'.

As with many of the world's great cities, it is difficult to identify a single architectural style representative of Paris as a whole. The tumultuous history of Paris, from its early development as an outpost of the Roman Empire through the destruction of the French Revolution and the impact of Baron Haussman's programme of urban-renewal, has resulted in a number of architectural face-lifts which have given rise to a plethora of grand monuments which comprise the city's unique architectural identity. Nonetheless, the multitude of architectural styles displayed in the fabric of Paris are united by one common factor: a desire for showing off to the rest of the world. The French kings' demand for a visual celebration of their power and glory initiated a tradition of architectural splendour which is proudly perpetuated by the *grands projets* of recent Presidents eager to promulgate the reputation of Paris as one of the most innovative European cities.

ARCHITECTURAL BEGINNINGS

As is the case with many of the world's greatest cities, the strategic impact of the river provided the raison d'être of Paris. The Seine flows through the city in a wide arch around two islands, the Ile-de-la-Cité and Ile-St-Louis. The first known settlers were the Parissi, a small Gallic tribe, who established a collection of fishermen's huts on the Ile-de-la-Cité. However, it was not until the Roman occupation of the site around 52-53 B.C. that there was any significant architectural development. Although Lutetia (the Roman title for Paris) was furnished with all the hallmarks of Roman civic life, few architectural vestiges of that occupation have survived to the present day. Two notable exceptions are the recently excavated, Gallo-Roman palatial baths underlying the present National Museum of Paris at L'Hôtel de Cluny and the amphitheatre, Arène Lutece, both situated on the Left Bank (Rive Gauche) of the river Seine. Although this area is now known as Le Quartier Latin, it was not so named because of any Romanesque associations but simply because it later became the intellectual and academic heart of Paris and Latin was the language in which lectures were presented.

LEFT An original plan of the Gallic city of Paris, then known as Lutetia.

BELOW The recently excavated palatial baths of the Emperor Julien.

GOTHIC SPLENDOUR

It was only in the 12th Century that Paris began to compete with Rome as a religious and political European centre. This was partly due to the strengthening of the French crown under the relatively stable rule of Philippe Auguste II and his devout successor, Louis IX. The latter, widely known as St. Louis, was the founder of the University of Paris, the Sorbonne, which received Papal authorisation in 1215 and was highly effective in promoting Paris as a centre of theological expertise. Although Philippe Auguste fortified Paris with city walls and the fortress on the site of the Louvre, it was with ecclesiastical structures, such as Saint Denis, Sainte-Chapelle and Notre Dame and the incorporation of the Gothic style that Parisian architects came into their own during the early Middle Ages.

ST DENIS

One of the earliest patrons of Medieval building was Abbot Suger (1081-1151), counsellor to Louis VI and VII, who masterminded the construction of the magnificent cathedral of Saint Denis. Suger wrote that he wanted "to make what is material immaterial", and thus introduced a host of new architectural advances: the pointed arch, flying buttresses and complex roof vaults. These features branded Saint Denis as the first truly Gothic edifice in Paris and pointed the way towards the towering conception of Notre Dame.

BELOW The magnificent aerial view of the Ile-St-Louis and Ile-de-la-Cité, with Notre Dame towering in the centre.

ABOVE The vast crypt inside the cathedral of Saint Denis.

RIGHT Saint Denis was one of the earliest truly Gothic medieval buildings in Paris.

NOTRE-DAME

Perhaps more than any other building, Notre-Dame is widely hailed as the symbol of historical Paris. The site of Notre-Dame at the heart of the Ile-de-la-Cité, has been regarded as sacred since Roman times when a temple dedicated to the god Jupiter was constructed. Although Notre-Dame was conceived by Maurice de Sully, Bishop of Paris, as early as 1163, its construction spanned two centuries of Gothic architecture. The cathedral is magnificent from every angle and is generally believed to represent the paragon of Early Gothic, religious architecture distinguished by pointed arches combined with flying buttresses. This technique permitted the replacement of heavy walls with glass in order to achieve a celestial elevation in contrast to the substantial style of Romanesque architecture. The cathedral was widely applauded and was emulated throughout Europe. Nevertheless, the history of Notre-Dame has not always been a glorious one. By the beginning of the 19th Century, the cathedral was in a poor state of repair and demolition was in the cards. This errant proposal was greeted by many with justified outrage. For instance, the celebrated French author Victor Hugo effectively petitioned for the renovation of "this vast symphony of stone" through the publication of his sensitive novel, *Notre-Dame de Paris*, in 1831.

SAINTE-CHAPELLE

Sainte-Chapelle was commissioned as a private chapel in 1248 for Louis IX, in his palace on the Ile-de-la-Cité. The main purpose of this prestigious gift to Paris was the provision of an appropriate resting place for the religious relics, the sacred Crown of Thorns and sections from the Crucifix, which he purchased from Baldwin II, Emperor of Constantinople in 1239.

The structural fabric of Sainte-Chapelle is second only to the beautifully illustrated, pictorial Bible in the chapel's exquisite stained glass cycle. The jewel-like character of the 15 glass panels is finely complemented by the lavish use of gold paint and the deep-blue ceiling laden with stars.

The overall effect is virtually transcendental and it is hardly surprising that during the Middle Ages the church was regarded as a gateway to heaven.

ABOVE 'A vast symphony of stone', one of the grandest symbols of architectural Paris, the cathedral of Notre-Dame.

ABOVE The gargoyles of Notre-Dame stand watch over the cathedral, keeping evil at bay.

LEFT The view from the Notre Dame belfry as seen by Henri Cartier-Bresson – Paris, 1953.

TOP The glorious Sainte-Chapelle, finished in 1248.

ABOVE The renowned stained glass windows.

Although the ecclesiastical splendour illustrated above was admired and imitated throughout France and beyond, Paris then suffered another cultural setback due to the upheaval caused by the Hundred Years War and the Black Death of 1348. For nearly two centuries, the French royal seat migrated from Paris to the Loire Valley. Therefore, in spite of the illustrious reign of the French king Charles V, it was Rome and Florence that became the leading lights of Renaissance architecture during the 15th Century. It was not until the return of François I to the Louvre in 1528 that Paris once again became a prominent political and cultural centre.

THE LOUVRE

The complex history of the Louvre provides us with a microcosmic view of Parisian architecture from the time of Philip Augustus II to the reign of Louis XIV in the 17th Century. The foundations of Philip's fortress, built around 1190, have recently been excavated and can be seen today whilst visiting the Musée du Louvre. Later, on the orders of Charles V, this fortress was rebuilt

as a royal chateau in 1370. One surviving representation of this, in its full glory, can now be seen in the background to the Month of October from the Limbourg brothers' illuminated manuscripts, *Les Trés Riches Heures*. With the return of Francis I to Paris during the 1520s, Charles V's chateau was no longer deemed appropriate as a royal residence and was destroyed. In its place rose the splendid façade of the Square Court, constructed by the architect Pierre Lescot at the heart of the Louvre with which many of us are familiar with today. The new palace followed the earlier plan, with the entrance on the east side, towards the town, and included the building of the west and south wings. Between 1667-70, Claude Perrault created the 183 metre long eastern facade, the elegance of which is now regarded as a highlight of 17th Century French classicism. During the 19th Century, Napoléon doubled the size of the Louvre, expanding the south wing and constructing the northern one to mirror it in a suitably imperialistic style.

In spite of these elaborate architectural projects, the history of the Louvre is not

ABOVE An illustration showing the Louvre fortress in all its glory after it was rebuilt by Charles V, from the Limbourg brothers' Illuminated manuscripts, *Les Trés Riches Heures*.

BELOW The foundations of the original fortress constructed under Philip Augustus II, c 1190.

unchequered. After Louis XIV shifted the royal residence to the Palace of Versailles, the rooms of the Louvre became inhabited by artists and squatters. By 1750 the palace was in such a bad state of repair that there was talk of tearing it down. Much to the chagrin of the French, it was the infamous lover of Henri XV, Madame de Pompadour, who saved the palace for posterity. She did this by appointing her brother as Superintendent of Buildings with the specific task of carrying out repair work on the Louvre. The Louvre now thrives as one of the world's largest and most prestigious art galleries and museums. François I's lavish patronage of Italian Renaissance art, particularly the work of Leonardo da Vinci, provides the centre-piece of the Royal Collection. Subsequent monarchs and ministers of state, notably Louis XIV, Richelieu and Mazarin, have all added their contributions to the collection. Interestingly, Napoléon was so obsessed with art as a status symbol that he renamed the Louvre, Musée Napoléon.

BELOW The Louvre, 1380, when it was being used as a royal chateau as ordered by Charles V.

ABOVE The historic bridge, Pont-Neuf, Ile-de-la-Cité.

NEXT PAGE One of the two public squares which were created under the rule of Henri IV – the Place des Vosges.

THE BEGINNINGS OF URBAN PLANNING

By the late 16th Century, Paris was one of the most densely populated capitals in Europe. The ancient bridges linking the Ile-de-la-Cité with the banks of the Seine had become too congested to cope with the rapid development of Paris as a mercantile centre. On 31st May 1578 the cornerstone for a new bridge, the Pont-Neuf, was inaugurated by François' successor, Henri III. Despite its title, today this is the only bridge to retain its original features. Throughout the 17th Century the Pont-Neuf was the place to be seen, primarily due to the fact that it had the first raised pavements in Paris. Furthermore, it was unencumbered by shops and provided an enchanting panoramic view of the Seine.

Under the rule of Henri IV, architectural confidence flourished due to an unprecedented desire for logical urban planning instead of wild growth. In 1609, the King ordered the creation of two public squares, Place des Vosges (Royale) and Place Dauphine. The Place des Vosges formed an elaborate nucleus for the developing Marais district on the Right Bank and to this day provides a striking example of civic urban planning. It is thought that the elegant arcades of this highly geometric square provided the inspiration for Inigo Jones' famous London piazza at Covent Garden.

ROME OF THE NORTH

Despite the changes described above, by the end of the 16th Century Paris largely remained a medieval city. It was only with the reign of Louis XIV, otherwise known as the 'Sun King', that a programme of modernisation was put in motion. As Superintendent of the King's buildings, Jean-Baptiste Colbert must take most of the credit. His administrative ideal was the Roman Empire with the city of Rome at its centre, the font of power, style, justice and cultural grandeur. Colbert drew the analogy of Paris as the equivalent centre of an imperial France, a sort of 'new Rome', and on this basis argued for the physical and cultural re-construction of the city. Moreover, Colbert believed that a great city is a modern city. The medieval wall was replaced by tree-lined boulevards such as the Champs-Elysées. The old city gates were replaced by triumphal arches, notably the Porte St-Denis which was directly inspired by those of Classical Rome.

This enlightened process of rational urban planning based on firm classical ideals continued throughout the subsequent reign of Louis XV (1715-74). Nowhere is this more

PLAN DE LA VILLE CITTE ET VNIVERSITE ET FAVXBOVRGS DE PA

6326 Paris - Porte Saint-Denis

ABOVE Porte Saint-Denis, one of the many classically inspired structures to appear in Paris under Jean-Baptiste Colbert.

RIGHT The Champs-Elysées – tree-lined boulevards were another priority during the reign of Louis XIV.

CHAMPS ELYSEES

ABOVE Jacques-Germain
Soufflot's Panthéon –
looking back at the
perfection of Greek
architecture.

evident than in Jacques-Germain Soufflot's Panthéon. This architect's stated aim was to return to the perfect harmonies of Greek architecture on a grand scale. The Panthéon's current status is a shrine to France's Greatest Men, including the 19th-Century writers Victor Hugo and Emile Zola. This Neo-Classical disposition continued through the turbulent years of the French Revolution and the subsequent rule of Napoléon I and is finely exemplified by architectural projects like the Arc de Triomphe, La Madeleine and the highly ordered Place de la Concorde.

THE REMAKING OF PARIS

During the 19th Century, Paris underwent numerous changes as prestigious new monuments, public buildings, roads, railway stations, and other amenities began to feature on the urban landscape. This was largely due to the endeavours of Napoléon III's Prefect of the Seine Department, Baron Georges Haussmann. Ironically, much of what we believe to be intrinsic features of Paris, the Eiffel Tower, the elegant tree-lined square and spacious boulevards, date only from the 19th Century. Pre-Haussmann Paris is now a matter of seeking out historical images and applying a degree of informed imagination. It can also be argued that Haussmann's process of urban renewal had an impact on the architectural fabric of Paris comparable with that of the French Revolution on France's political infrastructure.

Haussmann firmly believed that Paris did not have a hope of becoming a modern

thriving city as long as its inhabitants continued to dwell in the insanitary conditions vividly described by Victor Hugo in *Les Misérables*. His most visible legacy was the opening up of new thoroughfares and public spaces through a gargantuan programme of slum clearance and road building. Beginning in the city centre, Haussmann constructed 12 boulevards radiating from the axis provided by the Arc de Triomphe. Together with the proliferating rail system, these broad boulevards well and truly broke up the heart of old Paris. Furthermore, the new road system was only one part of Haussmann's plan to modernise Paris. With the assistance of the engineer Belgrand, he masterminded a comprehensive programme of sanitary improvements with the creation of a modern sewage system and the installation of gas supplies across the city. He supported a number of building projects using iron and glass as the main components of construction, notably the Paris Opera and the market place of Les Halles (destroyed in 1971). In addition the Gare du Nord and

BELOW Baron Georges Haussmann's new layout of Paris. The *etoile* (star) leads from the Arc de Triomphe at the centre.

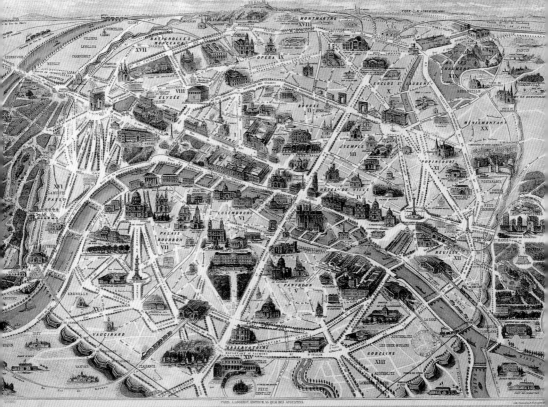

ABOVE A souvenir of *'Nouveau Paris'* showing the changes made by the modernisation of the city.

BELOW The Gare du Nord (train station) was opened during Haussmann's period of grand urban renewal.

Gare de l'Est were opened during the prolific Haussman period and provided fitting symbols for Napoléon's concept of grand urban renewal.

Although greatly appreciated by many of the city's inhabitants, there was a bitter reaction from a number of pre-Haussman devotees, notably Victor Hugo and Charles Baudelaire who argued, with some justification, that the destruction of 'Old Paris' had been far too wholesale and indiscriminate. For instance, 80 percent of the Ile-de-la-Cité was destroyed. Ironically, Haussmann's improvements did not succeed in deterring the social discontent that resulted in the political uprising of the Commune in 1871 which further contributed to the destruction of 'Old Paris'. The Louvre, the Palais de Justice and the Palais Royal were all damaged; the Hôtel de Ville and many of the old medieval streets of private residencies were obliterated. The cathedrals of Notre Dame and Sainte-Chapelle were also targeted but fortunately, those in charge of this operation could not actually bring themselves to descend to such wanton acts of destruction!

This bleak episode in the social history of Paris was followed by an extensive

programme of repair which launched the city into a prosperous era of industrial and economic exhibitionism. This period produced two brand new monuments that have become part and parcel of the popular notion of all that is Parisian: the Basilica of Sacré-Coeur (where it is alleged that there are prayers said around the clock to expiate the sins of the Commune) and the Eiffel Tower.

THE EIFFEL TOWER

This unforgettable sign of 19th Century ingenuity is now not only one of the most popular symbols of Paris but also one of the most familiar man-made landmarks in the world. The tower was originally built to impress visitors to the Universal Exhibition of 1889 and was only intended to occupy the Parisian skyline on a temporary basis. In addition to inspiring wonderment and acclaim, the sheer audacity of this lattice construction of iron girders attracted much aesthetic outrage and derision. Over the last 100 years it has been described as the 'tower of Babel', 'a giraffe', 'a metallic carcass' and a 'graceful pencil sharpener'.

ABOVE Advertising the Paris Exposition of 1889.

LEFT The grand church Sacré-Coeur looms over the houses of Montmartre.

RIGHT The universally acknowledged symbol of Paris – the Eiffel Tower overlooking the Seine.

MODERN PARIS BUILDINGS –
LES GRANDS PROJETS

French Presidents have been keen to remain at the cutting edge of arts and architecture. The 1960s witnessed the construction of La Défense, the "Manhattan style" district, which is one of the largest construction projects undertaken in Paris since the end of the Second World War and has been described as Haussmanesque in scale. The 26 skyscrapers, situated in this western part of the city, have forever altered the Parisian skyline and the view from the Louvre along the Champs-Elysées. The Grande Arche, the centre piece of La Défense, makes reference to the Parisian tradition of the Porte St-Denis and the Arc de Triomphe but also provides a monumental 'window into the future'.

In 1969, Georges Pompidou initiated the multi-purpose arts centre which is now one of the best known post-war buildings in Paris. Designed by an Anglo-Italian duo of architects, Richard Rogers and Renzo Piano, the Centre Georges Pompidou initially received much criticism and was nicknamed the 'arty oil refinery'. The innovative, 'inside out' architectural approach is a refreshing contrast to the austere appearance of many museums and galleries. For instance, the external colour coding is highly user-friendly; green – water pipes, yellow – electricity lines, blue – air duct and red – escalators and human passage ways. Outside in the Place Georges Pompidou, a variety of colourful street artists amuse onlookers in a manner copied by Covent Garden amongst others.

RIGHT The unique Pompidou Arts Centre designed by Richard Rogers and Renzo Piano.

BELOW La Défense business district maintains the theme of arches with La Grande Arche.

NEXT PAGE The new and highly modern surroundings of La Défense.

LA DEFENSE

ENTRE POMPIDOU

'Le Grand Louvre' is one of the most recent and controversial additions to Parisian topography. The towering glass pyramid was commissioned by President Mitterand in 1984, and, designed by the Chinese-American architect, I. M. Pei, it provides an unforgettable introduction to the Musée du Louvre. Many feel that the pyramid is out of keeping with its classical surroundings, yet if one bears in mind that the structure is closely modelled on the ancient pyramids of Giza, it just provides another architectural layer for future generations to discover. The old and new complement each other in providing an unforgettable architectural spectacle of which Paris, the champion exhibitionist, can be proud.

Paris is now preparing for the next big event on the horizon – a gigantic clock positioned in front of the Pompidou Centre which ticks off the seconds until the year 2000. One can only wait with anticipation for the architectural Grand Projet proposed to mark this momentous event.

LEFT The staircase and interior of the Louvre pyramid. The natural light adds to the atmosphere of modernity.

BELOW A striking combination of old and new – the pyramid with the original building in the background.

E GRAND LOUVRE

ART

Among the many art treasures to be found in the French capital, an amazing collection of Claude Monet's paintings of his garden at Giverny is housed in the Musée de l'Orangerie in the Tuileries, seen here in 1930.

Renoir at the Ball of the Moulin de la Galette. The Moulin Rouge and Toulouse-Lautrec reproduced in colour on coasters in a Montmartre souvenir shop. The mysterious charm of the Passage de l'Opéra or the haunting beauty of the Bridge of Suicides in the Parc des Buttes-Chaumont. The meanderings of the Surrealists through the streets of Paris, around flea-markets, in search of a magical fortuitous encounter. Giacometti's Montparnasse studio captured on camera by Brassaï as the neighbourhood artists while away the time at the Closerie des Lilas or at the terrace of the Coupole. Above the bar at the Café de la Palette, in Rue Callot, rows of palettes are the only memory of the artists who once drank there. And tourists ask to see Monsieur Sartre's chair at the Café de Flore, holding their maps of Saint-Germain-des-Prés, looking for traces of its 1950s intellectual and creative effervescence. For artists have indeed left their mark on Paris as much as the city on them. Myths, clichés and nostalgia: Gershwin's American in Paris meets Kafka and Orson Welles by the great clock of the Musée d'Orsay.

MONTMARTRE

The hill of Montmartre was originally scattered with windmills, pleasure gardens and bourgeois mansions. In the second half of the 19th century, a number of workshops were established there, attracting an increasingly working-class population, especially after Haussmann had cleared the city centre slums described by Zola in *L'Assommoir* to make way for his great boulevards. Circuses, cabarets, brothels and all manner of entertainment soon followed, drawing in a more 'respectable' clientele from the bourgeois area just south of the hill.

By the 1880s, many artists were also moving up to Montmartre, tempted by its cheap rents and buzzing activity. They turned to the subject matter at hand. Though the Impressionists are often associated with landscape painting, the Seine at Argenteuil or a garden at Giverny, they also dealt with contemporary urban subjects. Monet painted the bustle and steam of the Gare St. Lazare; Degas showed a melancholy working class couple in *L'Absinthe* or depicted launderesses hard at work. As for Van Gogh, he frequented Le Tambourin, a Montmartre cabaret where he organized several exhibitions. Toulouse-Lautrec moved to Montmartre in the 1880s, and his paintings and colour lithographs constitute the most celebrated record of the quarter's low-life: cabaret entertainers,

ABOVE The hill of Montmartre with its windmills, still a rural environment in 1860.

LEFT The Swiss sculptor and painter Alberto Giacometti outside his Paris studio in 1960.

BELOW A Van Gogh from his Paris period, of a woman in his haunt the Café Tanbourin, 1887.

ABOVE The newly-opened indoor dance hall at the Moulin de la Galette, 1898.

BELOW Renoir's painting of the outdoor gardens at the same venue, from 1876.

prostitutes and *poules de luxe*. When Renoir had depicted the Moulin de la Galette, he had provided an idyllic, almost country-like picture of a pleasure garden, with its factory workers and clerks dressed in their Sunday best to take their sweethearts out. Lautrec's world was the more hectic environment of the Moulin Rouge, a fake windmill which opened in 1889 complete with bars, dance halls and music-halls.

The artists of Montmartre participated fully in the cultural swirl of the *Belle Epoque* era. Lautrec exhibited with the Incohérents, a group of witty artists and caricaturists who gathered at the Chat Noir cabaret, and the Nabis collaborated on shadow-theatre productions at the Chat Noir. Nor could artists remain impervious to the radical debates of their time. In the 1890s, Maurice Denis, Vuillard and Bonnard shared a Pigalle studio with Lugné-Poe who ran the Théâtre de l'Œuvre, a theatre close to anarchist circles. Later, the Revue Blanche, an intellectual lighthouse, played a crucial part in the Dreyfus campaign of 1898; the Nabis not only designed front covers for the magazine, but they also held an exhibition in

its offices, at the foot of the Butte Montmartre.

A victim of its success, the area was gradually deserted by artists at the beginning of the 20th Century, and the closure of the Moulin Rouge in 1914 marked the end of the golden age of Montmartre. Now visitors still flock around the Place du Tertre; they go from one easel to another, nodding approvingly or sceptically at more or less competent caricatures or picturesque canvases. Artists wearing bérets jealously guard their spots, ruthlessly chasing away any 'unauthorized' competitor. . .tourists take a few photographs and make their way down the hill, glimpsing the sex-shops of Pigalle on the way back to the coach.

LEFT The most famous poster for the Moulin Rouge, a lithograph by Toulouse-Lautrec in 1891.

ABOVE The Moulin Rouge – complete with its fake windmill – soon after it opened in 1889.

ABOVE From the Musée d'Orsay, Paul Gauguin's painting 'Schuffenecker's Studio', 1889.

LEFT Paul Gauguin photographed in front of his canvasses.

BELOW Pablo Picasso – the artist at work in his Paris studio in 1929.

MONTPARNASSE

Even in the 19th Century, painters and sculptors had frequented the Montparnasse quarter where they found cheap studios and an active bohemia. Manet, Gauguin, Strindberg, Monet, Renoir, Bazille, Sisley and Whistler had been regular customers at the Café Guerbois. Generations of artists and writers also gathered at the Closerie des Lilas: Baudelaire, Zola, Ingres, and also foreign students who studied at the Beaux-Arts or in the ateliers of local masters. At the Closerie, one could hear the poets Max Jacob or Guillaume Apollinaire at public readings held under the aegis of Paul Fort, or attend animated debates on the modern art of Picasso, Braque, Derain or Modigliani; and a few years later, the Surrealists would take over the Closerie with a notorious 'Chahut' or 'riot' event organized to decry Paul Claudel. Modigliani also became a regular at Chez Rosalie. Rosalie Tobia, an ex-model, welcomed penniless Montparnasse artists in her little Italian restaurant in Rue de la Campagne-Première and let them pay with engravings and paintings. Utrillo once decorated one of the walls of her restaurant with a scene from Montmartre, as though to mark a transition and confirm the status of Montparnasse as the new artistic capital.

As for Gertrude and Leo Stein, they held court at the Dôme, where, in 1907, they meet Matisse and convinced him to found an academy of painting. One of the Steins' protégés at the Dôme was the young Ernest Hemingway, who later recorded that period of intense artistic activity in *A Moveable Feast*. After the Dôme and La Coupole, La Rotonde gradually became the symbol of Montparnasse. There, Lenin played chess

ABOVE The café La Coupole in Montparnasse, pictured on a postcard from 1925.

BRAQUE

with Trotsky and Picasso, Braque, Derain or Cocteau came to sit at the terrace, as did Soutine, Kisling and Pascin. The American intelligentsia of the *Années Folles* – Hemingway, Fitzgerald, Pound, Calder, Faulkner or Dos Passos – preferred to gather at the Select. The spirit of those roaring twenties was encapsulated in the sensual figure of the artist, model, singer and friend of the artists Kiki de Montparnasse.

From the beginning of the 20th Century, an increasing number of artists found studios in Montparnasse. In 1909, Modigliani left Montmartre and settled in the Cité Falquière studio-complex. Braque stayed on in Montmartre, whereas Picasso followed the exodus to Montparnasse. Sculptors Henri Laurens and Jacques Lipchitz settled there, a stone's throw away from the atelier in which Archipenko taught his students. Nearby, in 1910, an art school was founded for Russian students who didn't speak French. The area of Montparnasse was most determinedly cosmopolitan.

Most legendary among studio-complexes is La Ruche. 'The Beehive' was built from fragments of a Pavilion at the 1900 Universal Exhibition, and housed 200 artists as well as a theatre run for a time by Louis Jouvet. The list of Ruche artists reads like a Who's Who of

ABOVE The cubist pioneer Georges Braque (1882-1963).

RIGHT A typical Braque still -life, 'Violin' from 1912.

ABOVE The French painter
Fernand Léger (1881-
1955) in his studio.

RIGHT Americans in Paris:
Writer Gertrude Stein (left)
in 1937, and the novelist
F. Scott Fitzgerald.

LA RUCHE

ABOVE Russian painter
Marc Chagall (1887-1985)
with his regular model
Bella in 1934; he fled from
Paris to the USA during the
Occupation.

BELOW 'Bather', a Picasso
from 1928, when he was
mainly based in Paris.

early 20th Century French and Ecole de Paris art. Fernand Léger moved there in 1908 and stayed until WWI. At one time or another, Rouault, Lipchitz, Alexandre Archipenko, Ossip Zadkine, Henri Laurens, Modigliani, Diego Rivera, Soutine and Chagall all had studios there. Every week, a little old man would wheel his cart over from the Rue des Rosiers (the traditionally Jewish quarter in the Marais area), to sell sausages and vodka to the many Jewish artists from Russia and Poland who lived at La Ruche. Most of them were to leave during WWII, along with the German artists. In 1970, La Ruche was declared a National Monument, thanks to a vigorous campaign led by Chagall and by writer and Culture Minister André Malraux. It thus escaped destruction by property developers, was thoroughly restored and is now the home of 80 or so artists of various nationalities.

After WWII, many artists, including Manessier, gravitated around the studios of the Rue de la Grande Chaumière. Another group was involved in the activities of the American Center, on the Boulevard Raspail, which for a few decades was a hot-bed of Franco-American avant-garde in the fields of art, theatre, dance, jazz and poetry. Today, the site is occupied by a striking glass building designed by architect Jean Nouvel to house the Cartier Foundation for Contemporary Arts, which puts together an idiosyncratic and inventive exhibition programme.

Even though Montparnasse remained a place of predilection for artists, by the end of the war, the scene had shifted imperceptibly towards Saint-Germain-des-Prés.

ART

47

PARIS

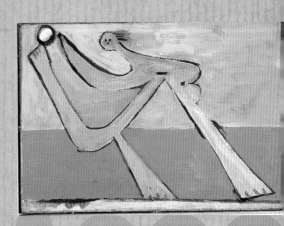

SAINT-GERMAIN-DES-PRÉS

In Saint-Germain too, the café life was an integral part of the quarter's intellectual, musical and artistic effervescence. Before the War, Les Deux Magots was frequented by poets Eluard, Desnos, Crevel, and the enigmatic figure of Antonin Artaud. Meanwhile, at the Brasserie Lipp one could rub shoulders with literary giants like Valery, Gide or Claudel. During and after the War, Le Café de Flore took over: Sartre, who had published *Being and Nothingness* in 1943, was joined at the Flore by novelist Simone de Beauvoir, Albert Camus, Jacques Prévert and Raymond Queneau.

Music was very much part of the Saint-Germain experience. Paris had traditionally been a haven for black American jazz musicians who could escape the colour bar and achieve artistic recognition; American saxophonist Sidney Bechet thus played at the Vieux Colombier while the French writer and musician Boris Vian played the trumpet at the Club Saint-Germain. At the Rose Rouge or the Tabou, one could catch sight of that template of Parisian existentialism, the actress and singer Juliette Greco.

Artists, critics and intellectuals exchanged ideas. Some like Poliakoff or Deyrolle met up with Atlan in Galatchi's boutique on the

ABOVE Albert Camus, the novelist, dramatist and essayist – a leading name among French intellectuals.

BELOW The Café de Flore in the early 1950s.

BECHET

ARTRE

TOP French jazz musicians including Claude Luter (far left) with the American Sidney Bechet (far right) at Paris' Vieux Colombier club.

ABOVE The leading French philosopher Jean-Paul Sartre (right) engaged in debate with Joseph Keller in a Paris café in 1958.

KANDINSK

ABOVE A painting by
Wassily Kandinsky (1866-
1944) from 1912 entitled
'Deluge II'.

Boulevard Saint Germain; others attended lectures at the Geography Room, or met at La Hune, a Bookshop cum Gallery which showed paintings, engravings and books by Hartung, Ernst and Michaux among others.

In liberated Paris, museums and galleries were throbbing with activity. The first Autumn Salon was held in October 1944, only weeks after the Germans had left the city and was aptly titled the 'Salon de la Libération'. New Salons like the May Salon, the Salon of New Realities or the Salon of Painters Witnesses of their Times concentrated on new trends.

Influential Right Bank gallerists included René Drouin who opened in Place Vendôme just before WWII, in collaboration with Leo Castelli. After the war, Drouin showed Wols, Fautrier and Dubuffet, and stored the latter's collection of 'Raw Art'. New galleries opened on the Right Bank, several of them run by women like Lydia Conti and Colette Allendy; Denise René was one of the first to support hard-edge constructivist abstraction and her gallery is still very active, with premises on the Right Bank as well as in Saint-Germain.

In Montparnasse, Pierre Loeb's gallery was established in the 20s, as was Jeanne Bucher's, and specialised in Kandinsky and other abstract painters. Some Saint-Germain galleries, like the Galerie de Breteau, were also created before the war; they were joined in the late 40s by the likes of Nina Dausset who, as early as 1951, perceived an international abstract trend and exhibited painters like de Kooning or Jackson Pollock alongside the Italian Capogrossi, the Canadian Riopelle and artists working in France like Bryen, Hans Hartung or Wols.

The main post-war current, non-geometric abstraction, concentrated on textures and gestures, expressing the tensions and drama of its epoch: Fautrier's series of Hostages conveyed the horror of his war-time experience, and his thick impastoed surfaces were metaphors for battered and debased flesh. Similarly, Samuel Beckett saw the paintings of his friend Bram van Velde as ways of figuring the impossibility of expression. Other abstractionists of the 'informal' current included Dubuffet, Hartung, Mathieu, Michaux, Riopelle, Nicolas de Staël and Wols. The figurative current was mainly represented by

ABOVE The instigator of 'Art Brut', Jean Dubuffet with a sculpture made from volcanic lava in 1955.

ABOVE 'Yellow, Grey, Black' by the pioneer of abstract expressionism, Jackson Pollock, who with his 'drip' pantings was revered in Paris as much as in his native America.

RIGHT Drawing for a kinetic work of art by Jean Tinguely in 1969 which was to feature in the spectacular Fountains ensemble outside the Pompidou Centre.

Giacometti and Germaine Richier. Jean Genet and Jean-Paul Sartre both saw in Giacometti the archetype of the angst-ridden existentialist artist; Richier's work is also haunted by ideas of destruction, dissolution and spiritual malaise.

In the 40s, Braque was painting subdued interiors and still-lifes while Picasso shocked his audience with his renewed vitality. Meanwhile, other movements emerged, such as Cobra, defended by the Galerie Loeb, or the Lettriste movement. As for the Surrealists, they were back from their war-time exile in America and organized numerous exhibitions in Saint-Germain, even as the Galerie Maeght put on the legendary 1947 International Surrealist Exhibition. Until the mid 1950s, the Paris art scene positively vibrated with energy and variety.

NEW REALISTS AND NEW REALITIES

In the late 50s, a group of artists associated with galleries like Denise René or the Galerie Beaubourg, reacted against the more lyrical, and by now almost academic, elements in post-war abstraction. For the 'Young critics' section' of the First Paris Biennale in 1959, Pierre Restany selected one of Yves Klein's monochromes. At the 1960 May Salon, César exhibited three compressed cars. At the second Paris Biennale, Arman showed one of his 'bin-accumulations'. A school was born, manifesto and all.

Far from rejecting all representations of reality, the New Realists aim to appropriate reality in its most concrete aspects, including the secretions of consumer society. In order to create such forms of urban poetry, the affichistes Villeglé and Hains rip posters off the walls of Paris and displace these fragments of banale reality into the context of art. Similarly, Daniel Spoerri 'traps' fragments of daily reality in his quirky 'Tableau-Piège' assemblages, and Jean Tinguely recycles scrap-metal into sculptures. One of the most popular pieces of '*nouveau réaliste*' municipal art is the Fountain-ensemble outside the Pompidou Centre, a collaboration between Tinguely and Niki de Saint-Phalle, each fountain an individual character with a mechanical life of its own.

The movement as such only lasted less than four years, but produced some of France's most interesting and respected

ABOVE A model poses in an outfit by Paris designer Yves Saint Laurent in 1966, with a sculpture by Niki de Saint-Phalle.

RIGHT The Fountain ensemble outside the Pompidou Centre with works by Tinguely and Niki de Saint-Phalle.

artists, Yves Klein among them. For 'Le Vide' in 1958, the Iris Clert Gallery was emptied ('*vide*') and painted white; on either side of the door stood two Republican Guards in full attire; blue cocktails were served to visitors who were shown in small groups, as crowds waited in the Rue des Beaux Arts, queuing to experience Klein's 'immaterial pictural sensibility' – or to scoff at it. Soon afterwards, Arman filled the same gallery with detritus to create 'Le Plein' ('full'). And in March 1960 at the International Gallery of Contemporary Art, Klein used three female models as live paint-brushes: they covered their naked bodies with Klein's distinctive blue before pressing themselves against sheets of white paper. Twenty musicians and singers accompanied the performance in front of a hundred bemused spectators.

ABOVE An assemblage by Arman of paint brushes on canvas, 'Pure Epic', 1988.

RIGHT 'Cosmogeny', a work by the iconoclast and innovator Yves Klein.

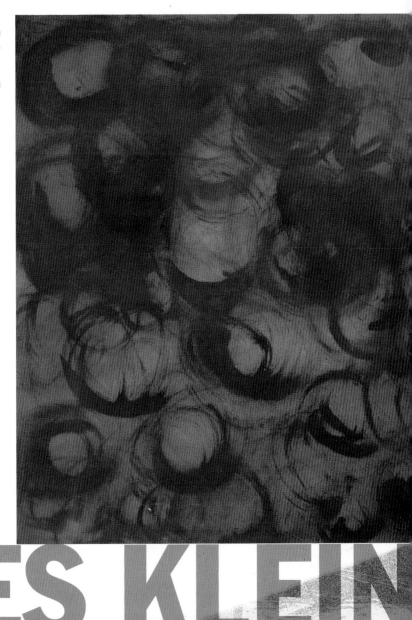

YVES KLEIN

THE CONTEMPORARY FLÂNEUR

Art has historically been a vehicle through which royal and then presidential power left its stamp on the capital. When the Pont Neuf was finished in 1606, Henry IV placed at one end of it a statue of himself on horseback (paid for by raising a special tax on wine). Throughout the *Ancien Régime*, many artists benefited from royal patronage and were allocated studios in the Louvre Palace. The successive Paris Great Exhibitions were another means of expressing national grandeur and identity. More recently still, President Mitterrand initiated his '*Grands Travaux*' among which are the controversial pyramids at the Louvre and the Great Arch in La Défense business quarter, which echoes the Arc de Triomphe in its scale and drama. Across the street from the Louvre, Daniel Buren's columns in the courtyard of the Palais-Royal seem to stress the government's will to link past and present art.

Great museums are landmarks across the city. If the Louvre, the Musée d'Orsay, the Musée d'Art Moderne de la ville de Paris, the Picasso Museum or the Pompidou Centre sometimes feel like art supermarkets, other museums are less daunting. The Orangerie boasts an outstanding display of Monet

BELOW Daniel Buren's sculptures in the courtyard of the Palais-Royal, like the Louvre pyramid in stark contrast to their setting.

Waterlilies, and paintings by Soutine and the
School of Paris; the Jeu de Paume was
refurbished a few years ago to present
contemporary art exhibitions. Monet's last
paintings, donated to the state by the artist,
are to be found at the Musée Marmottan.
The Jacquemart André Museum, a 19th
century private mansion, staggers the visitor
with its monumental staircase, winter garden
and an astonishing collection of Flemish and
Italian Renaissance art.

Small museums are like gems scattered
throughout Paris. The painter Gustave
Moreau, who had taught Matisse and
Rouault, bequeathed his home-studio to the
state, along with the thousands of works it
contained. The Maillol Museum was founded
by the artist's ex-model Dina Verny to present
works by the Nabis, Maillol himself, and a
selection of avant-garde artists ranging from
Duchamp to Kabakov. The Espace Electra, a
former power-station, organizes innovative
contemporary art shows. The Zadkine
Museum is a peaceful haven, and the
Delacroix Museum nestles behind the church
of Saint-Germain-des-Pres.

The private galleries are myriad, ranging
from the upmarket Galerie Lelong, by the
Elysée Palace, to the smaller galleries very
recently created near the New National

TOP Manet's 'Nympheas'
on show at the Orangerie.
photographed in 1930.

ABOVE Claude Monet at 80
painting 'Nympheas', from
the garden at Giverny, 1920.

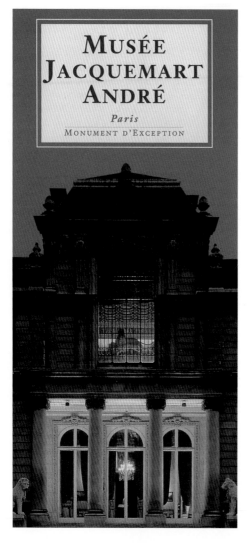

MUSÉE
JACQUEMART
ANDRÉ
Paris
MONUMENT D'EXCEPTION

ABOVE A leaflet for the
Musée Jacquemart André
which houses classical art
and furniture on the
Boulevard Haussmann.

PREVIOUS PAGE The
magnificent main hall in
the converted railway
station, Musée d'Orsay.

Library in south-eastern Paris. Since the 80s, and partly in the wake of the Picasso Museum opening, private galleries have mushroomed in the Marais, drastically changing the character of this traditionally Jewish and working-class quarter, attracting chic boutiques and trendy bars – many of the latter catering for the gay community. Starting with galleries closer to the Pompidou Centre, such as Daniel Templon, Galerie du Centre or Galerie de France, one can amble towards the heart of the Marais and the galleries around the Rue Debelleyme, where Marian Goodman exhibits Ruscha or Richter and Thaddaeus Ropac exhibits Warhol, Gilbert & George or Sturtevant, while in the Rue Vieille du Temple Yvon Lambert presents New York artists Julian Schnabel, Jenny Holzer or Nan Golding.

On the Left Bank, too, each gallery has its own personality. The Galerie 1900*2000 harbours treasures of minor Surrealist art; Jeanne Bucher is faithful to abstract painters like Nicolas de Staël; Lara Vincy is renowned for her Fluxus exhibitions; Samy Kinge for his collection of Victor Brauner's works; and Darthea Speyer has consistently strived to introduce offbeat American artists such as Peter Saul or Ed Paschke.

Monet, Cézanne or Toulouse-Lautrec came from 'la Province', the School of Paris consisted mainly of cosmopolitan Parisians, and several Nouveaux Réalistes were Niçois. Artists converged towards the capital in search of artistic kinship and recognition. It has become commonplace to say that after the War America's economic supremacy extended to the arts and that, in the words of critic Serge Guibault, 'New York Stole the Idea of Modern Art'. One might argue that at the present moment, artistic creativity is no longer associated with any one city in particular, but shared out between various international venues. Paris is certainly no longer the centre of artistic creation; nevertheless, showing and looking at art is deemed part of a precious tradition and, as the Pompidou Centre's recreation of Brancusi's studio reminds us, the artistic memory of the city is also preserved in places which bear the mark, albeit somewhat nostalgic, of a presence.

ABOVE The interior of the pyramid which forms the present-day entrance hall to the Louvre museum.

ASHION

Paris, as well as being the prime centre of international haute couture fashion, has long been a veritable paradise for the stylish consumer shopping for clothes.

Text: Elaine Deed

On Sunday, July 12th, 1998 the streets of Paris swarmed with football strips and rang with blaring horns. The city renowned for its chic, was a sea of blue, red and white as the French celebrated their World Cup victory. Poiret, Dior and Vionnet must have been spinning in their graves. For a day, the last thing on the minds – and backs – of the people in Paris was fashion. Of course, the French are as fiercely competitive and nationalistic when it comes to fashion as the World Cup. Paris is fashion. Its streets are the architects of *chic*, the word that in just four letters encapsulates that well-groomed stylish *je ne sais quoi* of Catherine Deneuve, Coco Chanel, Ines de la Fressange – and the Francophile beatnik, Jean Seberg, wandering down a Parisian boulevard selling the New York Herald Tribune in Jean Luc Godard's 1960 film, *À Bout de Souffle*.

LA MODI

Yet, it's a contentious issue as to who currently holds the trophy in the international fashion league. Paris? London? Milan? New York? Paris has always been a formidable player, determined to retain its image as the centre of fashion even if it has meant encouraging foreign players onto its team from time to time.

If you look down the long list of members of the elite Chambre Syndicale du Prêt à Porter des Couturiers et des Créateurs de Môde you will find many an adopted overseas designer who has been embraced by the French fashion industry.

Since Englishman Charles Worth set up in the late 19th century, Paris has been the home to international talent and maintained its position as the hub of fashion.

Today, many of the major French fashion houses have become international design hybrids. Among the most headline-making alliances of the late 90s, there are the British designers, Stella McCartney, John Galliano and Alexander McQueen creating collections for Chloe, Christian Dior and Givenchy respectively; Americans Marc Jacobs at Louis Vuitton and Michael Kors at Celine; the Italian-based Narciso Rodriguez doing the Loewe line; Israeli Alber Elbaz designing for Guy Laroche; and, of course, the German-born Karl Lagerfeld at Chanel.

For foreign designers there is still the kudos of working in Paris, the city synonymous with fashion.

FAR LEFT A true style icon of *chic*, Catherine Deneuve – seen here in 1965 – was, like Bardot before her, a protégé of Roger Vadim.

LEFT The ultimate 'sex kitten', Brigitte Bardot epitomised French allure in her films and personal life through the 50s and 60s.

ABOVE Jean-Paul Belmondo and Jean Seberg in Godard's iconographic 1960 movie *À Bout de Souffle* (*Breathless*).

BELOW RIGHT Leslie Caron made her film debut with Gene Kelly in *An American In Paris* (1951) and typified the gamine 'elfin' look.

Since the French Revolution of 1789, Paris, rather than the royal court at Versailles, has been the style-setting centre of France. From Paris in the late 18th century came les Incroyables, the dishevelled dandies, and les Merveilleuses, the post Revolution leaders of the social and fashion scene led by Mesdames Récamier and Tallien.

HOME OF COUTURE

Charles Frederick Worth created the first ever couture salon in 1858, reinventing the traditional role of the dressmaker. Based in the Rue de la Paix, he started with a staff of 20. Within 10 years when the great Paris Exhibition was held in 1867, he had around 1200 employees and was dressing not only royalty and nobility but also trainloads of Americans who arrived with empty trunks to fill with Worth's frocks.

But it wasn't long before French designers set up to rival Worth. Paul Poiret, one of the first, was far more than just a dressmaker. He was an integral – and sometimes tortured – lynchpin between the then disparate worlds of art and fashion.

ABOVE Inside the House of Worth in 1907, dressing the mannequins for a fashion show.

ABOVE Charles Frederick Worth (1825-95), the British-born father of modern haute couture.

'Am I mad,' he once said, 'when I try to put art into my dresses, or when I say that couture is art?'

He is credited with revolutionising the feminine shape at the beginning of the century. He freed women from the ubiquitous corset and created a whole new look inspired by Africa and the Orient.

His enthusiasm for all things to do with style was legendary. In one year, 1911, he founded the Ecole Martine for interior design, launched the first couture perfume, Rosine and threw a huge party for all Paris high society. 'I am a Parisian from the heart of Paris,' he wrote in the opening line of his memoirs in 1930. He was born on 20th April, 1879 in the rue des Deux-Ecus, the son of a cloth merchant. Unfortunately when he died on 28th April, 1944 he was penniless, having banked on his creative couture vision rather than the new commercial trends.

Rags have created riches but, equally, riches to rags is a common story of everyday designer life in the fickle world of fashion. Although he didn't end up in rags, the great Cristobal Balenciaga who came to Paris from Spain in the late 30s, gave up couture and fashion once and for all in 1968 with the famous declaration, 'it's a dog's life'.

ABOVE A Worth creation from 1920: 'Esperez', an evening dress featured in *Gazette du Bon Ton*.

BELOW An illustration from *Gazette du Bon Ton* of costumes by Paul Poiret, June 1914.

COCO CHANEL

The story of Coco Chanel reads like a film script – which, in fact, it became in *Chanel Solitaire* in 1981. Gabrielle Coco Chanel started her climb to fame working in a hat shop in Deauville 71 years earlier.

Although she was brought up in an orphanage, she was attracted to the rich and famous and was soon moving in high social circles. With the support of her dashing English lover, Boy Capel, she opened two shops of her own in Deauville and Paris selling millinery, blouses and dresses.

Significantly she did not follow the staid and starched fashion of the top couturiers but started making clothes that she deemed more comfortable to wear in jersey – a fabric, until then, more normally associated with underwear. By 1918 she was making cardigans and twin sets and adapting men's clothing including sweaters, shirts and blazers to wear over plain long skirts or wide-legged pants. Soon her signature flat black bows, gilt buttons, sling-back sandals and gilt-chained bags became recognised symbols of the new, decadently relaxed style of dressing.

She reopened in Paris after the war in 1919, the same year that Boy Capel was tragically killed in a car crash and in 1921 she launched the world's most famous scent, Chanel No 5. Her philosophy that clothes should be unrestricting and wearable defined a new era in fashion. She never deviated from uncluttered and unfussy styling. Famously, she declared, 'Let us beware of originality: in couture it leads to costume'. Within 10 years her annual turnover was 120 million francs and her designs were copied everywhere although, unlike other couturiers, Coco Chanel didn't mind being plagiarised. Imitation, she maintained, was the sincerest confirmation of success. Yes, Coco Chanel had come a long way from the orphanage. She now had a Hollywood lifestyle with rich lovers including the Duke of Westminster, artistic friends such as Jean Cocteau and Pablo Picasso, and a famous clientele that included the Hollywood glamour queen, Gloria Swanson. Then came the war and the long shadow of German occupation fell on the streets of Paris. Coco Chanel closed her doors in 1939 at the start of World War II re-opening in 1954 at the age of 71.

ABOVE Gabrielle Coco Chanel – in one of her own outfits– in 1937.

RIGHT The post-war Chanel revival typified 60s chic – here a suit from 1964.

BELOW From 1910, a magazine cover featuring a hat by Gabrielle Chanel.

COMŒDIA illustré

M.lle LUCIENNE ROGER
S LE MARIAGE DE M.lle BEULEMANS
GRAND SUCCÈS DE LA RENAISSANCE

CHAPEAU, CRÉATION GABRIELLE CHANEL
21, RUE CAMBON.

Showing a collection in Paris, again, was a brave move not only because of the risk of being regarded as out of touch with fashion but also because, after the war, her liaison with Nazi officers led to her arrest as a collaborator and exile in Switzerland.

For a while it looked like her gamble had failed – the French received her first collection with little enthusiasm, a punishing coolness for her disloyalty. But Chanel had not lost her touch – or instinct about – what women want to wear. Her looser more relaxed silhouette came as welcome relief from the pinched waist 40s look. She captured the chic mood of the 50s with her tweedy jersey suits and pearls – and was once again queen of the fashion world until she died, alone in her suite at the Paris Ritz, in 1971.

ELSA SCHIAPARELLI

She may have been Italian, but Schiaparelli was every stylish inch a product of Paris. She arrived with her daughter in 1920 from New York having separated from her husband. Her first successful design was a black sweater with a trompe l'oeil white bow which was seen and ordered in quantity by a store buyer. She opened a shop called Pour le Sport in 1928 and by 1938 she had her salon and boutique in the Place Vendome.

That innovative first black sweater was the blueprint for her design success. Witty and eccentric details were her trademarks. Although dubbed 'that Italian artist who makes dresses' by rival Coco Chanel, it was her artistic flair that made her famous, using friends in her circle including Dali, Bérard and Cocteau to design fabric and accessories.

Among her most memorable creations was the famous hat shaped like a shoe and the suit with lip pockets designed with Salvador Dali. There were also bags that lit up and played a tune when opened, and the brilliant Bérard pink that became known as 'shocking'. She also named her perfume Shocking, which, of course, didn't come in any ordinary bottle but in the silhouette of a tailor's dummy.

Like Coco Chanel, she closed her doors during the Second World War but, unlike her tenacious competitor, her subsequent relaunch from 1945 to 1954 was not a success. Elsa Schiaparelli retired from fashion and spent her last days in Tunisia and Paris until she died in 1973.

ABOVE Elsa Schiaparelli in London's Hyde Park in 1935, promoting her then revolutionary trouser suit.

LEFT From French *Vogue*, November 1938, the surrealist inspired ad for Shocking perfume.

BELOW LEFT A creation by Schiaparelli in the French publication *Modes & Travaux*.

ABOVE A drawing by the famed illustrator Sam for Dior's debut New Look collection of 1947.

RIGHT Christian Dior personally supervises one of his models in a New Look dress.

CHRISTIAN DIOR

It was Christian Dior who quickly brought the fashion focus back to Paris immediately after the war. Backed by Marcel Boussac, the fabric millionaire, the 42 year old Dior opened his salon and showed his first collection in 1947. The amount of fabric used in his new sweeping skirts, which measured up to 25 metres, was condemned as wasteful so soon after wartime rationing, notably by Sir Stafford Cripps, President of the British Board of Trade. There were even anti-Dior demonstrations – a young woman wearing Dior was photographed being attacked in the Rue Lepic by a couple of outraged elderly women.

But Dior's shapely silhouette caught on quicker than you could say 'New Look'. Women welcomed the return to femininity and frivolity created by full skirts, nipped in waists and tight bodices. As Dior himself concluded the next season when the amount of material and underpinnings used did not deter his army of customers, 'When hearts are light, mere fabrics cannot weigh the body down'. Sadly, only 10 years after rocketing to fame, Christian Dior died, succeeded by the young Yves Saint Laurent.

YVES SAINT LAURENT

If he were not already Saint Laurent, the French would surely have canonised him by now. Yves Saint Laurent is the unofficial patron saint of fashion in Paris. Algerian born, he won first prize for a drawing of a dress in a fashion contest sponsored by the International Wool Secretariat and studied at the Chambre Syndicale school in Paris, before he started working for Christian Dior in 1955. He was only 21 when he became head of the House after Dior's untimely death.

His collections for Dior, although feted by the press, shocked the conservative couture world. There were alligator skin motor cycle jackets, mink coats with sweater sleeves and turtlenecks under mannish flannel suits among the controversial looks of his last collection. This may have been why, while he was called up into the Algerian army, in 1960 Dior replaced him with Marc Bohan. But Saint Laurent returned after only a couple of months, discharged because of ill health. Although bitter that he had no position at Dior, he decided to open his own salon with

DIOR

YVES SAINT LAUREN

ABOVE Yves Saint Laurent in 1961, not long after his departure from the House of Dior, 1961.

TOP RIGHT Catherine Deneuve modelling a Saint Laurent ready-to-wear dress in his Paris boutique.

RIGHT A catwalk shot from the YSL haute couture collection for Autumn/Winter '96.

his business partner Pierre Bergé in 1962. A shrewd move as it turned out.

The rest, including the designs that have become museum classics such as the safari suit, the Mondrian dress, the see-through blouse and Le Smoking, his famous dinner suit for women, is fashion history.

He captured a whole new generation as customers – here was a designer catering for the daughters instead of the traditional matriarchal couture clients. His were clothes synonymous with the bohemian Left Bank and the hip beaches of St Tropez.

But, for Saint Laurent designing clothes has always been more about creating style that endures rather than making one-season-wonder looks for victims. 'Fashion passes quickly,' he wrote in the book *Yves Saint Laurent* published by The Metropolitan Museum of Art for his 25th anniversary retrospective, 'and nothing is more pathetic than those puppets of fashion outrageously made up one day, pale the next, pleated or ironed stiff, libertine or ascetic.'

The designer who introduced women to so many great fashion looks also states, ironically, 'I wish I had invented blue jeans: the most spectacular, the most practical, the most relaxed and nonchalant. They have expression, modesty, sex appeal, simplicity – all I hope for in my clothes.'

THE RISE OF READY-TO-WEAR

The House of Saint Laurent is now a huge empire. Like many a major designer, Saint Laurent's name has become a highly valued commodity in the French fashion industry.

It started in the 60s – for Saint Laurent in 1966 when he launched his Rive Gauche ready-to-wear label. Fashion was suddenly taken over by the mass youth cultural revolution. You no longer had to be affluent or middle-aged to wear the latest designer creations. In Paris it brought about the rise of Courrèges, Ungaro and Cardin – along with an unprecedented rise in hemlines.

Today Pierre Cardin is the king of product licensing. The story of his success is a lesson in fashion marketing. Following his initial indisputable claim to fame with his Space Age collection, in 1964 a trend milestone in fashion history, he shamelessly exploited his growing status in the hedonistic 60s. In 1968 he issued his first licence contract outside

fashion – for porcelain china. Two years later, Espace Pierre Cardin – the theatre, restaurant, cinema and exhibition hall opened in Paris. In 1977 he launched Maxim's Boutique, the start of a whole new line of products, prior to taking control of the celebrated Maxim's restaurant in Paris.

Now, at the age of 76, he has a global business with 850 licences. As he told *The Times*, 'I can live my life entirely within my empire. I can sleep on my sheets in my hotel, dine in my restaurant, wear my own clothes, sit on my sofa.'

By the 70s, the closed shop created by the couturiers with their twice a season presentations was being penetrated by new designers arriving via alternative routes to the fashion scene. Claude Montana, Thierry Mugler, Azzedine Alaïa were not couturiers. They were the first band of ready-to-wear designers to infiltrate the Paris couture circle. And they were not going to show their collections in gilded salons.

It was the start of the fashion circus of ever more spectacular designer catwalk shows. From a sedate week spent perched on gilt chairs in hushed salons, the magazine and fashion editors found themselves at off-beat venues such as the Salle Wagram in avenue de Wagram and the Cirque d'Hiver in rue Amelot. Here, late at night, they were pushed and shoved, their tickets checked by burly

ABOVE From February 1967, a model wears a very 1960s day dress by Courrèges.

RIGHT Fantastic plastic hit the catwalks in the Pierre Cardin 1969 collection.

BELOW Models parade at a Paris presentation of dresses by Pierre Cardin.

COURREGES UNG

guards, along with packed hoards of fashion groupies worshipping the new heroes of style.

And gone were the days when no one was allowed to so much as sketch a seam while watching a couture show, so paranoid were the designers of mass retail imitations. By the 80s, hordes of photographers, film and video cameras were recording every stitch on the catwalks. The upbeat tempo of the Paris shows featuring loud music and gyrating models, set the pace for fashion worldwide. The French were magnifique. And then came the Japanese. Acknowledging the fact that Tokyo was too far a trip to ever attract the fashion pack, designers from Japan showed up in Paris – and stayed. Yohji Yamamoto, Comme des Garçons and Issey Miyake were the big threesome who changed the face – and shape – of fashion in the early 80s. Not since Poiret's oriental look, had the Far East had such an influence on western fashion. The models wearing the new Japanese collections wore no smiles, sombre shades and strangely folded fabrics. Overnight, fashion editors changed into black.

Paris continued to flourish. The top designers were producing their own ready-to-wear labels plus diffusion collections, jeans collections, menswear and fragrance lines. In fact, soon the ready-to-wear designers had created companies with all the fame and trimmings of the couture but a far wider and

LEFT A sensational, though highly impractical, outfit from Issey Miyake in the Autumn/Winter '89 collections.

BELOW From the Spring/Summer Paris shows of 1997, a dress by Comme des Garçons.

MAMOTO
SSEY MIYAKE
MME DES GARÇONS

ultimately more lucrative clientele.

Some spread themselves thin. Too thin, perhaps. Karl Lagerfeld, the prolific German designer, was designing his own label, plus Chanel, Fendi and Chloe. Including couture, he was doing 12 collections a year.

By the mid 90s, Paris had embraced a whole host of international designers including the British Vivienne Westwood, Rifat Ozbek and John Galliano.

The French quickly recognised the attraction of the young outré talents from Britain. When Hubert de Givenchy hung up his white couturier's coat for the last time, the embroiderers and seamstresses of this exclusive world may have thought their days were as numbered as the dwindling amount of made-to-measure creations sold.

But it was Bernard Arnault, head of the huge luxury goods conglomerate, LVMH, who came to the rescue. Asking John Galliano for Christian Dior and appointing Alexander McQueen to create for Givenchy was a stroke of fashion genius, breathing new life into the couture workshops of Paris.

Be outrageous, he told them before their shows, knowing that the huge media coverage created by their presentations however over the top, would help publicise the labels at all levels and boost sales of the brands world-

ABOVE A piece of Lagerfeld fantasy from the Spring /Summer shows in 1993.

RIGHT Karl Lagerfeld makes an appearance at the 1993 Autumn/Winter Paris collections.

RIGHT A Givenchy coat, jump suit and top that appeared in 1997.

wide. And it worked. Old houses have risen from the fashion history books, shaken off the cobwebs and, once again, attracted the world attention to Paris.

And so couture has been given a new lease of life. With the colourful French designers, Jean-Paul Gaultier and Christian Lacroix (also with LVMH) and, more recently, the Italian Donatella Versace, doing couture collections in Paris, the icing looks like staying on the gateau for some years to come.

But if anyone actually thought Paris had exchanged fashion status for football stadium during the summer of 1998 they need not have worried.

How did the World Cup Final kick off at the Stade de France? Not with football chants but with a £2m spectacle featuring 300 international models wearing 40 years of French fashion by Yves Saint Laurent.

Vive la Mode.

ABOVE British designers Alexander McQueen (left) and John Galliano, both of whom have established themselves in Paris fashion houses.

RIGHT A class act: a Galliano creation from the Christian Dior collection of Autumn/Winter 1997.

FESTIVALS

There was celebration on the streets of France's capital as the country was freed from the Nazis by the Allies – May 7th 1945 – but for centuries, Paris has been a city of enjoyment as the many festivals and holidays show.

Text: Diana Craig

Renowned for its elegance and sophistication, Paris offers a kaleidoscope of seasonal revels, festivals, fairs, exhibitions and parades, to suit every taste and interest. Since the city's history goes back to pre-Roman times, some of these festive traditions are centuries-old, while others are relatively new, the creation of the culturally diverse, vibrant and modern city that Paris is today. Some reflect important dates in the religious calendar or in the city's turbulent historical past, while others are purely for entertainment and enjoyment.

CHRISTIAN FESTIVALS

The first seasonal event of the year is, of course, the New Year celebration – but it is impossible to separate this festival from the one that immediately precedes it: Christmas. In Paris, Christmas effectively begins on 4 December, when the *Crêche de Noël* – the traditional nativity crib – is assembled in a tent in the *parvis de Notre Dame,* outside the famous cathedral. Notre Dame provides the perfect focus for the city's celebration of the most important feast in the Christian calendar, for it is not only a religious landmark for Parisians, but a historical one too. Although building on the cathedral did not begin until 1163, the site on which it stands, the Ile-de-la-Cité, is the place where, in about 250 BC, a Celtic tribe called the Parisii first settled, and gave the city its name.

Notre Dame again takes centre stage in the Christmas festivities when Parisians throng the cathedral for the midnight mass which begins at 11pm on Christmas Eve. Traditionally, they return home after this to enjoy *réveillon,* or Christmas dinner. France is justly famous for its cuisine, and *réveillon* includes a range of delicacies such as oysters, *pâté de foie gras,* black pudding or *boudin,* game, and goose or turkey stuffed with chestnuts and truffles, followed by a richly dark confection called *bûche de Noël,* a very superior form of chocolate yule log.

A week after the excesses of Christmas, the population of Paris rouses itself again for more celebrating. On 31 December, known as Réveillon or the Fête de la St-Sylvestre, crowds of revellers pack the Champs-Elysées to see in the New Year, while on New Year's Day itself spectators can enjoy La Grande Parade de Montmartre, a parade with floats and girls in fancy dress.

L'ILLUSTRÉ
DU PETIT JOURNAL
ET SON SUPPLÉMENT AGRICOLE
GRAND HEBDOMADAIRE POUR TOUS

TOUS LES
DIMANCHES

50

8-1-33

LE JOUR DES ROIS

Noël... Le Jour de l'An... Et le Jour des Rois !... Semaine de fêtes familiales... Celle-ci est une des plus charman...
Petits et grands s'amusent à trouver dans la galette traditionnelle la fève qui confère une brève et joyeuse roya...

(Voir l'article pag...

ABOVE The family enjoys a huge meal during the Feast of Kings. The King and Queen are seated in the centre.

ABOVE The intricate little ceramic lucky charms, baked into cakes for the festival.

The Christmas festivities are not yet over, however, for on 6 January or Twelfth Night, Paris celebrates the Fête des Rois, literally the Feast of the Kings. On this day, thousands of *galettes des rois* – little frangipani pastry cakes made with cream, almonds and sugar – are consumed in the hope of finding the beans or tiny lucky charms hidden within them. Whoever finds one in his or her *galette* puts on a cardboard crown to become king or queen for the day, and can select a consort of his or her choice. The roots of the Fête des Rois go back centuries, to pre-Christian times, in fact. The date on which it is celebrated, 6 January, was once – until 11 days were removed from the calendar to align it more correctly with the solar year – the day on which Christmas fell.

In medieval France, the 'King of the Bean' was chosen by exactly the same method as his modern counterpart, and was in turn descended from the Roman King of the Bean, a figure connected with the Saturnalia, the seasonal revels that took place in ancient Rome around the end of the year.

Public religious observance continues in spring when, on Good Friday, the Chemin de la Croix, or Stations of the Cross, is enacted by the Archbishop of Paris. These 'stations' are the 14 stages that traditionally make up Christ's journey from condemnation to death to crucifixion and entombment, and a crowd follows the Archbishop as he performs them, starting at the bottom of Montmartre and going all the way up the steps to the basilica of Sacré-Coeur.

Later in the year, the Feux de la St-Jean celebrates another key figure in the Christian story – St John the Baptist, whose feast day falls on 24 June. Fireworks are let off along the Seine, while another firework display at the futuristic La Villette park also marks this midsummer period. Finally, on 15 August, Notre Dame again becomes the focus for religious celebration with the Fête de L'Assomption, or Feast of the Assumption. This is the day when Roman Catholics honour the Virgin Mary and the assumption of her body into heaven to be reunited with her soul. To mark this event, a procession follows a statue of the Virgin as it is carried around the Ile-de-la-Cité.

Immediately after Halloween, All Saints' Day on 1 November honours souls of another

ABOVE St John the Baptist baptising Christ, Pol de Limbourg, 15th Century.

ABOVE An official portrait of Louis XVI, by Antoine François Callet.

BELOW The execution of Louis XVI, 21 January 1793, today the French remember this day in a variety of ways.

kind for this is when Parisians go to visit the graves of dead relatives and friends. The day has been designated a public holiday.

POLITICS

If the ancient traditions of the Roman Catholic Church are still alive and well in Paris, the city does not forget its political past either, nor the great Revolution that put an end to the rule of the monarchy. On 21 January 1793, two years before the end of the Revolution, King Louis XVI lost his head on the guillotine; on the Sunday nearest this date, monarchists attend a commemorative mass for the king at the Chapelle Expiatoire in the 8th *arrondissement*. Republicans however, have a different way of marking the event – with black humour, they tuck into a dish of *tête de veau,* or calf's head.

The political theme continues with the Fête du Travail on 1 May. A public holiday observed even more fervently than Christmas or New Year, this – like May Day or Labour Day – is a celebration of the working man (and woman). Except for the Eiffel Tower, all other monuments and museums are closed, rallies and marches parade through

ABOVE A 1936 poster for the French Labour Day – Fête du Travail.

ABOVE Celebrating July 14th. The poster dates from 1945, which would have meant a double celebration after WWII.

RIGHT Dancing in the streets on Bastille Day.

the city past the Bastille, and lilies of the valley are sold in the streets.

Early June sees a display of state pomp as the president's regimental guard flings open its doors to the public on the Boulevard Henri IV in what is known as the Portes Ouvertes à la Garde Républicaine. Horses and regimental weaponry and brass are all on show. But the most important political holiday of the year must be Le Quatorze Juillet – Bastille Day – on 14 July. Part of the fortifications of Paris, the Bastille had for years been used as a state prison and was seen as a symbol of royal repression. By 1789, various factors had combined to bring popular discontent with the monarchy and ruling class to boiling point and, on 14 July, a huge crowd answered the call '*aux armes*' and stormed the Bastille, thus setting in train the French Revolution and the country's successful – if bloody – transition from kingdom to republic.

In Paris, celebration of this turning point in French history begins on the evening of 13 July with dancing and parties. The following day is a public holiday. At 10am, Parisian hearts swell with national pride as, watched by crowds of spectators and to the roar of jetplanes overhead, the French President leads a spectacular military parade from the Arc de Triomphe to the Place de la Concorde. The day finishes with a firework display at the Trocadéro gardens.

The President again officiates on Armistice Day, the public holiday on 11 November when the dead of both world wars and other wars are remembered. In honour of their memory, the President lays wreaths on the Tomb of the Unknown Soldier at the Arc de Triomphe. In France, the flower of remembrance is the cornflower, because its colour recalls the blue trousers worn by infantrymen in World War I. It would presumably also have flowered in the fields of Flanders like the familiar poppy.

ABOVE French soldiers line up for the Armistice Day Parade, Paris.

BELOW The original Armistice – French and British soldiers and civilians celebrating the good news – 1945.

COSMOPOLITAN PARIS

As well as being proud of its French history, Paris is of course a cosmopolitan and multi-cultural city, and this is reflected in various festivals throughout the year. In late January or early February, people in Chinatown around the Avenue d'Ivrey celebrate the Nouvel An Chinois, the Chinese New Year. Brightly coloured Chinese dragons weave their way through the streets, to the accompaniment of loud cymbal-banging.

Later in the year La Goutte d'Or, the Arab and African district of the city, erupts in a joyous explosion of ethnic music. La Goutte d'Or en Fête, which takes place in early July, features local as well as established musicians offering a feast of rap, reggae and raï.

ABOVE Lanterns and dragons – festivities at the Chinese New Year celebrations in the 19th Century.

BELOW Laying wreaths on the tomb of the unknown soldier, at the Arc de Triomphe.

The lively sounds of Africa warm the winter months, too, with another musical event in late December at the Théâtre Gérard Philipe. Africolor presents traditional and modern African music from all over the continent, and culminates in an all-night party on Christmas Eve – an alternative for anyone who didn't make it to the midnight mass at Notre-Dame.

For those unmoved by African and Arabic rhythms, there are plenty of other musical events to choose from. Two that are a must for classical music lovers are the Musicora, a festival of classical music that takes place at the Grand Palais in the second week of April, and, from mid-June to mid-July, the Festival Chopin à Paris. This consists of a series of piano recitals, themed around the music of Chopin, held in an appropriately elegant setting – the Orangerie in the Parc de Bagatelle, Bois de Bologne.

Late March and early April offer lovers of jazz, blues and soul a treat in the form of Banlieues Bleues, a musical festival which attracts big names and is held in and around the St-Denis area, while on 21 June, Paris celebrates the longest day of the year with free musical performances all over the city. There is, in Paris, something for every taste, from rock and reggae to salsa, steel bands, and string quartets.

ABOVE Polish pianist and composer, Frédéric Chopin – drawing by Eugène Delacroix, 1838.

RIGHT The score for 'Trois Nocturnes' by Chopin, whose music is celebrated every year at the Festival Chopin à Paris.

Musical extravaganzas continue in high summer when the Parc de la Villette plays host to the humorously named Halle That Jazz festival, or Jazz à la Villette, a musical event which has gone from strength to strength since its beginnings in the mid-1980s. The park where it is held was once the site of several slaughterhouses, but where these stood are now a complex of ultra-modern buildings, the brainchild of the Swiss architect Bernard Tschumi who has transformed a fairly unpromising location on the outskirts of Paris into one of the city's most exciting places to visit. While the Cité des Sciences et de l'Industrie in the north of the park offers state-of-the-art science exhibits, the Grande Halle, Cité de la Musique, Hot Brass, Conservatoire de Musique and Théâtre Paris Villette in the south are the festival's venues where, in early July, jazz buffs come to hear well-known jazz, blues and Latin players as well as lesser-known experimentalists.

Parisians clearly have plenty of stamina, for hot on the heels not only of La Villette but of the Bastille Day revels too comes Paris, Quartier d'Été . Beginning on 14 July and continuing through to 15 August, this is effectively a month-long garden party, when Parisians take to the open air to enjoy a rich mix of performance arts – concerts, theatre,

TROIS NOCTURNES pour le PIANOFORTE composés et dédiés à son ami Ferdinand Hiller par FR. CHOPIN. OP. 15.

ABOVE The French are a nation of festival lovers — street parties and celebrating have been a part of life for years. A magazine cover from 1936.

dance, circus – all served up in the parks of the city, including the Jardins du Luxembourg, the Jardin des Tuileries, and the Place du Palais-Royal.

THE ARTS

If summer has its own festival, autumn – not to be outdone – has one, too. This, the Festival d'Automne, takes Parisians through from 15 September past the shortest day of the year to 31 December. It is more highbrow than the city's summer festival, and features challenging avant-garde theatre, music and dance. One of the festival venues is the Théâtre de la Ville which stands in the Place du Châtelet, the site of a medieval prison, and which is one of a pair of twin playhouses designed by Davioud in the 1860s. Once owned by the great French actress Sarah Bernhardt, it now hosts some of the best contemporary dance in Paris.

It would be remiss of Parisians, whose country has produced some of the century's most notable movies, not to honour the film industry. Accordingly, for about a week from the end of March, inhabitants of the French capital are able to attend the Festival du Film de Paris, which runs a selection of around 50 new, international films. Unlike the Cannes film festival, which is full of glitter and glamour and only accessible to an élite, the Paris equivalent is a much more egalitarian and interactive affair which gives the general public the chance not only to see the pick of new movies but also meet some of the directors and stars.

Parisians are noted for their taste in all the arts, and their love of fine things has spawned one of the city's most idiosyncratic traditions. In early June, antiques dealers of the now-fashionable 6th *arrondissement* host the curiously named Les Cinq Jours de l'Objet Extraordinarire. For five days, each antiques shop adorns itself with flowers and makes a special display of a particular object, chosen for its relevance to a single, shared theme such as 'the five senses'. Ironically, the 6th *arrondissement* was the home of Parisian café society, and the former beat of such great literary, artistic and intellectual figures as Arthur Rimbaud, Jean-Paul Sartre and Simone de Beauvoir until the area moved upmarket, putting it out of the price range of impoverished writers and artists and, some would say, destroying its old character.

RIGHT The streets of Montmartre are adorned for the grape harvest.

BELOW Arthur Rimbaud, in Paris, along with other intellectuals of the day in a painting by Fantin-Latour, 1872.

BOTTOM Antiques on display during Les Cinq Jours de l'Objet Extraordinarire.

ABOVE AND RIGHT More celebrations and fancy dress in Montmartre for the grape harvest during the Fête des Vendanges à Montmartre.

FETE DES VENDANGE

ABOVE The last remaining vineyard in Paris, which provides the grape harvest in early October.

THE GREAT OUTDOORS

Thoroughly urban though they are, Parisians still recall a more rural past, which they remember with the Fête des Vendanges à Montmartre which takes place on the first weekend of October, and celebrates the grape harvest from the city's last surviving vineyard in Montmartre. The residents enter enthusiastically into the festive spirit, by donning historical costume, and a parade as well as bands ensure that the whole event goes with a swing.

The call of the great outdoors infects Paris at other times of the year, too, in the form of a variety of sporting events. As in London and New York City, the Marathon has become one of the landmarks of the city's year. Held in early April and lasting two hours from 9am–11am, it involves around 20,000 runners, racing to see who will be first to cover the course from the Champs-Elysées to Avenue Foch.

A couple of weeks later, less energetic types set off from Paris in their vintage cars in the Tour de France Auto, heading for La Rochelle. Then, in late May professional stars of the tennis world begin to arrive for the two-week-long Internationaux de France de Tennis – the French Tennis Open Championship.

Back in the world of the amateur sportsperson, the end of June witnesses the Parisian version of the humble egg-and-spoon race – a tongue-in-cheek event and an example of the French sense of humour. In the Course des Garçons et Serveuses de Café, over 500 stereotypical but genuine French waiters and waitresses, clad in formal black, wearing white aprons, and bearing trays of drinks, compete with each other in a race

RIGHT The Paris Marathon as it draws to an end on the Avenue Foch.

TOUR DE FRANCE
1899

DE KNYFF sur
PANH

across 8 kilometres to and from the Place de l'Hotel de Ville. Any contestant that breaks a bottle or glasses is out of the race.

As the sporting year winds to a close, Parisians can enjoy two of the most famous events of that year. The first is the end of the Tour de France in late July or early August when spectators crowd the Champs-Elysées to see which of the returning cyclists, having survived the gruelling course of the world's most famous cycling race, will be first past the winning post. A month or so later, on the first Sunday in October, another great racing tradition comes to Paris. This is the Prix de l'Arc de Triomphe, the celebrated and fashionable horse race that takes place at Longchamps in the Bois de Boulogne, and provided artistic inspiration for the Impressionist painter Manet.

Like any other large city, Paris has its share of fairs and exhibitions. From the end of March to the end of May, citizens can literally enjoy 'all the fun of the fair' when the Foire

01 PARIS. — *Aux Courses.* — *Devant les Tribunes.* — LL.

ABOVE The stands
and spectators at the
Longchamps race, c 1900.

RIGHT Capturing the spirit
of the race, *Horse Racing*
by Edouard Manet, 1872.

BELOW RIGHT The Prix de
L'Arc de Triomphe
Longchamps, 1998.

ONGCHAMPS

ABOVE A 17th Century performance of *The Two Coaches*, shows Scaramouche and Harlequin in dispute, 1695, Foire St-Germain.

LEFT A comic opera taking place during the Foire St-Germain, St-Germain-des-Prés, 1750s.

RIGHT A rather more contemporary scene at the Foire St-Germain – a brass band plays on the street.

du Trône, France's largest funfair, comes to town, setting up home in the city's biggest park, the Bois de Vincennes. Here, families, young people, and the young-at-heart can take their pick from all the usual fairground attractions, ranging from ferris wheels and haunted houses to fortune tellers and bearded ladies. In June, the Foire St-Germain, a descendant of the medieval fair in St-Germain-des-Prés, offers stalls, music, theatre, and poetry readings.

Another, more modern tradition at which Paris excels is the trade fair, for the city is a world leader in this field, hosting over 500 such events each year. Many are held at the Paris-Expo, the French capital's largest exhibition centre at the Porte de Versailles. Depending on personal interest, Parisian exhibition addicts can come here to any number of fairs, from the Salon d'Agriculture, a massive agricultural show at the end of February, or the Foire de Paris – a kind of 'lifestyle' event featuring interior design, food, wine, sport and leisure exhibits in early May – to the Mondial de l'Automobile, October's motor show, or December's boat show, the Salon Nautique International de Paris.

Those of a more cultural inclination are not left wanting either, for October also sees the staging of the Foire Internationale d'Art Contemporain (FIAC), a huge exhibition of contemporary art in which well over 100 French and foreign art galleries participate. Renovation of the Grand Palais, FIAC's former venue, has meant that the exhibition has had to move to the Espace Eiffel Branley in the 7th *arrondissement*.

With such a crowded calendar, it is a wonder that Parisians get any time for rest. Nor is the list above exhaustive, for new traditions are always evolving to be added to the old – all of which makes Paris not only one of the most elegant cities in the world but also one of the most vibrant and exciting.

BELOW A 1930 advertisement for the Foire de Paris.

FOOD & D

Confitures extra

Kg 190 — 200

Abricot
Kg 195 — 210

Although the Parisians invented 'nouvelle cuisine', there are some aspects of their eating and drinking habits that are uniquely French and very traditional. A little girl walks home with a fresh baguette.

Text: Jackum Brown

French cooking is renowned as one of, if not actually the finest cuisines in the world – and Paris is its gourmet capital. Food in France is very regional: dairy produce and apples dominate in Normandy, olive oil, tomatoes, basil and fish dominate in Provence, while *charcuterie* and chestnuts reign supreme in the Ardèche. *Choucroute garnie* is a typical dish from Alsace: *piperade* (scrambled egg with red peppers and tomato) and Bayonne ham are famous Basque dishes. Brittany is known for shellfish and classic recipes such as *boeuf bourguignonne* and *coq au vin* originated in Burgundy. All these regional cuisines and more are to be found in Paris together with scores of cafes, brasseries and restaurants which reflect the different ethnic communities such as North Africans and Vietnamese who have made the city their home.

LEFT Still an important part of the Parisian lifestyle. The market place remains popular among everyday shoppers.

ABOVE Paris' Le Consulat restaurant brightly illuminated at night.

BELOW RIGHT La Grenouille is situated on the Left Bank, its owner Roger is known as the rudest and most eccentric restaurateur in Paris.

CAFÉ SOCIETY

Officially about nine million people live in Paris, but in reality the city is far smaller than that. The ring road, known as the Périphérique, encloses the true city, which is divided by the river Seine, thus giving rise to the Right and Left Banks and the whole place is divided into 20 areas or *arrondissements*. If you care to, you can walk almost everywhere, which is really the best way to get to know any city. When you get tired, the excellent public transport system is there to help you. Or of course you can stop at a café or brasserie for a rest, a drink and a good look at the people passing by.

Sadly, in Paris as in the rest of France, traditional cafés are closing down at a frightening rate. Most people simply do not have the time any more to sit for hours, drinking coffees and reading their way from one end of the newspaper to the other. And as rents rise it becomes more and more difficult to make a living from a simple café. There will always be a good number of PMUs *(Paris Mutuel Urbain),* however, which are betting shops with a café/bar attached and *Bar/Tabacs* are the same type of place. There you can find soft drinks, coffee, hot chocolate or tea

Filet de hareng
Salade composees
Salade Mixte
grillades garnie
Steack Frites
Steack Au Poivre
Entrecôte garnie
Faux Filet garnie
côtes d'agneau garnie
fromage Au choix

(though this is usually a tea bag in hot, rather than boiling water). In the morning you will normally be able to have a croissant, a brioche, a *pain au chocolat* or a *pain au raisins* which, together with a large *café creme,* makes a good start to the day.

Draught beer known as *pression;* a glass of kir, which is white wine with a little black currant liqueur; pastis; various vermouths; and other typically French aperitifs such as Pineau de Charentes, a delicious blend of cognac and wine, are just a few of the alcoholic drinks available in a Paris café/bar.

The French only drink wine with their meals and in general, French women drink very little indeed, preferring mineral water. Men like to drink whisky, which is considered chic, port is drunk as an aperitif rather than a digestif and at the end of a meal (when the cheese is always eaten before the dessert) a good, sweet, white wine or a digestif such as Armagnac or Poire William would usually be drunk in preference to a sweet liqueur such as Grand Marnier, which would be more commonly used in the confection of some deliciously rich desserts.

In Paris despite the fact that numbers of traditional cafés have closed, new places, including the ethnic restaurants and fast food joints as well as bistros and bars open all the time. Sandwiches are a popular and inexpensive snack all over the world in one form or another – in France they are filled baguettes without butter, unless specifically requested, in which case it will be extra cost.

ABOVE One of the many old bars, Montparnasse.

LEFT Displaying the menu, Ile-de-France, Paris.

ABOVE Enjoying a drink in a Parisian bar – a favourite pastime.

A CULINARY TRADITION

The French rarely invite guests to eat in their homes, normally only family and very close friends have that privilege. They are, however, very hospitable and gregarious and tend to invite guests to restaurants instead – thus one is made very much aware of the significance that eating and drinking with friends and colleagues have in the social fabric of France in general, and Paris in particular.

As the pace of life has sped up in France, some of the old traditions of shopping and cooking are fading. Many women have very demanding jobs and are simply not interested in shopping around carefully for the perfect vegetables in the market and the gleaming *loup de mer* (sea bass) on the fishmonger's slab and they certainly do not want to come home in the evening and spend a couple of hours cooking. Even so, everyone still does some form of daily food shopping, even if its just going to the *boulangerie,* where you choose your flute or baguette, specifying one that has been well or lightly browned, as you please. Traditionally baguettes would be bought three times a day, before each meal. Nowadays people tend to buy a longer lasting loaf such as a *pain rustique* as well as their baguettes, so they can eat fresh bread without having to keep rushing off to the bakery.

Freezers in the home are still quite rare, thus ready cooked foods are gaining in importance in France, as in Britain, not only in the home but in restaurants as well, with frozen *frites* and vinaigrette in little plastic sachets beginning to make an appearance. However if you use your eyes and your nose and look for a likely spot, you can still eat very well in establishments of all sorts and within all price ranges.

Guide Michelin started using one star to denote particularly good restaurants in 1926. One star meant '*Bonne table dans sa catégorie*' or roughly speaking 'good food of its type'. In 1931 they added two stars meaning 'excellent, worth a detour' and three stars meaning 'one of the very best in France, worth a special trip'. Still hugely influential, the new edition of the *Guide* is eagerly awaited every year.

In recent years another guide, *Gault Millau,* has been giving the *Guide Michelin* stiff competition and is very widely used in France. It recommends restaurants that serve

RIGHT AND BELOW There are a huge number of patisseries, bakeries, delicatessens and *fromageries* all over Paris – all display their mouth-watering goods in abundance.

BELOW 'At the Restaurant', a caricature on the cover of the magazine *Rions!*, 1909.

ABOVE A fashionable and sociable pastime – The Casino de Paris, 1945.

truly wonderful food but in less august surroundings, as many people prefer to eat in more relaxed atmosphere these days, and many of the Michelin starred restaurants are overly hushed and chi-chi.

HAUTE CUISINE

If you have decided to spend some serious money on an evening out at one of the capital's best restaurants make sure you book well in advance. Somewhere like the three star Grand Véfour in the Rue de Beaujolais (metro Palais Royal) is often booked up for at least a week in advance, but then it is one of the most beautiful restaurants in the world. Napoléon Bonaparte, Victor Hugo and Colette (who lived nearby) are but three of its impressive list of famous former clients – if you want to sit at one of their tables you just have to ask. Built in 1784 the painted ceiling, gilt mirrors and luxurious sense of history are well worth taking a look at, even if you are not going to eat there.

Most restaurants have a menu which is at a fixed price as well as the à la carte menu, although in very fine establishments the fixed price menu may only be available at lunchtime. These establishments also usually offer *menu dégustation* or *menu gastronomique* which enables you to eat all their specialities

Lucas-Carton is another top restaurant. Situated in the Place de la Madeleine (metro Madeleine) it is a wonderful example of *belle époque* decor. However unlike Guy Martin's classic food in the classic surroundings of Le Grand Véfour, the chef, Alain Senderens, is a modernist – indeed he practically invented 'la nouvelle cuisine'.

Le Jules Verne is the restaurant in the Eiffel Tower that gives you not only chef Alain Reix's fabulous shellfish and veal dishes, but also the most spectacular views over Paris and the bridges crossing over the Seine. This is a hugely popular restaurant with both locals and tourists alike, and has to be booked weeks in advance even though it is open every day of the week.

La Tour d'Argent at Quai de la Tournelle (metro Pont-Marie) also has fantastic views of the Seine and Notre Dame, which can be enjoyed as you eat their famous Tour d'Argent duck. As with Le Jules Verne, make sure you book a table by the window.

BELOW A menu from Eiffel Tower restaurant Le Jules Verne, 1889.

Naturally while Parisians hold good food very dear to their hearts, and love to go to a first class restaurant every now and then, like everyone else they eat at home much of the time, and eating at home means shopping for food. Many people find shopping in supermarkets is convenient and for many items it is less expensive (though also less good quality) than shopping elsewhere.

THE STREET MARKET

However, food markets in France are an ancient tradition and are still extremely popular. Probably the busiest day is still Sunday – this is traditional all over France because not only is it a day off for most people but also more importantly almost everything is shut on Mondays. There are around 60 open air food markets in Paris and about a dozen covered markets; many are open from 8am – 1pm and 4-7pm, Tuesday to Saturday and Sunday mornings. Some only operate two or three days a week. The market in Boulevard Raspail (metro Rennes) is on Tuesdays and Fridays and on Sundays it turns into the Marché Biologique devoted to selling organically grown or raised produce.

The market at Rue Mouffetard (metro Monge) is very good fun and all the fruit and vegetables are gorgeously displayed. Ernest Hemingway shopped here as did Josephine Baker and it is one of the oldest markets in the city. This is part of the Left Bank area which is full of students from the Sorbonne and other colleges, so the atmosphere is very easy going and light-hearted. The Café Mouffetard is a great place to have breakfast or a snack and watch the lively crowd. The Marché d'Alligre (metro Ledru-Rollin) is another very good market and one of the cheaper ones. It is open every morning except Mondays and consists of both a covered and an open air market. It is a great place for ethnic items and has a wide range of exotic fruits and vegetables as well as bric-a-brac, second hand clothes and so on.

For centuries Les Halles was Paris' central market, covering a huge area. Nowadays, as with the Covent Garden and Billingsgate markets, it has been moved out of Paris towards Orly and what remains is situated on the pedestrianised Rue Montorgueil (metro Chatelet or Les Halles) and in fact even now lots of restaurants still get their supplies there.

ABOVE Fresh artichokes at a Paris market.

ABOVE A fresh fruit and vegetable stall from the Rue Mouffetard market.

BELOW An old favourite ingredient, much used in French cuisine – garlic.

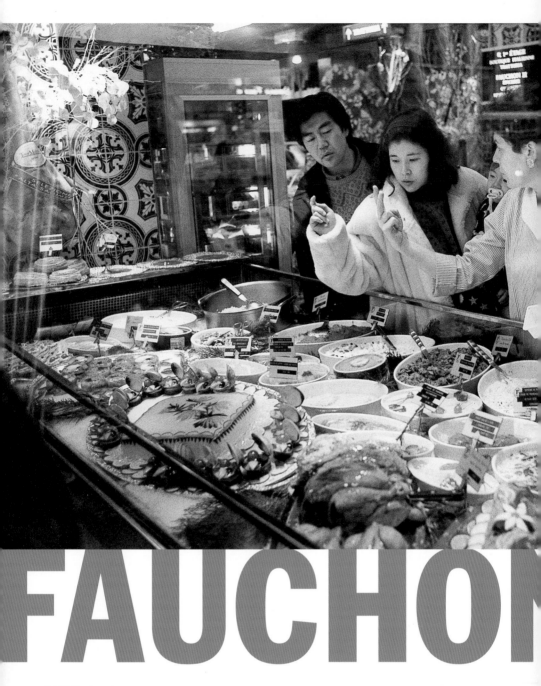

FAUCHON

ABOVE The best known
food store in Paris –
Fauchon – at Place
de la Madeleine.

You may feel that the huge underground shopping mall and the garden that replaced the remarkable iron and glass pavilions that covered the old markets were not a good change, but you can always console yourself with a visit to the Patisserie Stohrer which was started in 1730 by the then queen's chef and is still as famous as ever.

Not far away on the Rue Coquilliere is the equally famous restaurant Au Pied du Cochon, which is open 24 hours a day, and is always full of action. You might want to try their house speciality, which is of course, stuffed roasted pigs trotters – they are reputed to sell 80,000 portions a year! Paris is very good at late night eating: at 3.00 am you can leave a party and almost instantly find somewhere to drop in and have a nourishing onion soup to help you on your way home.

SHOPPING FOR FOOD

Moules and *frites* is another Parisian tradition – there are stalls everywhere, near the mainline train stations, in the Place de la République, on many street corners – and this is a delicious, filling and inexpensive meal. Crepes with all sorts of different stuffings, from savoury to sweet, oysters in season, *bavette* (steak cut along the grain rather than across), shallots and *frites,* all of these French traditions are enjoyed by locals and visitors alike. As well as the many markets in Paris, there are also innumerable excellent food shops, from butchers and bakers to specialists selling chocolate, or cheese, truffles or caviar and everything in between. Busy Parisians can produce a fantastic dinner party in no time by cheating and buying everything from a *traiteur.*

The best known food store in Paris is Fauchon at Place de la Madeleine and it sells just about everything. Its window displays are worth a special trip and once tempted to enter, you'll find it hard to leave without buying something, if only for the experience. It is of course expensive but you do not have to buy much and you can spend a long time admiring the beautiful presentations. Nearby is the Maison de la Truffe which sells truffles and truffle related products such as sauces and vinegar, which unlike the real thing, are not too expensive. Right here you will also find shops that exclusively sell caviar, foie gras, cheese and chocolates.

ABOVE Sweet delicacies freshly made and sold on the premises.

BELOW Achat de Chevaux, a butcher's shop.

ACHAT DE CHEVAUX

ABOVE An old-fashioned
all-encompassing grocery
store in the heart of Paris.

BELOW An impressive
cheese board with a variety
of high quality cheeses.

La Maison du Miel, in the same area, is another uniquely French shop. There you will find more types of honey than you would believe including about 30 from France alone and you can taste as many as you like before you decide on the one for you! You can also find all sorts of other items that are honey based, from cake to hand cream and none of it is going to break the bank. In every market in the French countryside you will find a little stall selling local honey and honey products but here its all under one roof.

On the Ile-St-Louis is the most famous ice cream place in Paris, selling around 100 different flavours of sorbet and ice-cream. Berthillon is closed on Mondays and Tuesdays, but the rest of the time there is almost always a queue.

The French like sweet things as you can tell from the delicious looking tarts and pastries in patisserie windows, and they are very fond of chocolate. There are many marvellous shops selling confectionery of various kinds – La Maison du Chocolat's own chocolate is excellent and they make cakes and eclairs as well as individual chocolates. Christian Constant on the Rue du Bac is a chic, modern chocolate maker whose bitter chocolate sells to many a famous name.

Fromageries – cheese shops – abound, and are absolutely fascinating. All year round, different French cheeses come into their best form and people often ask the advice of their cheese merchant before they make their

SPECIALITE
DE
TARTES CHAUDES
SALEES
A TOUTE HEURE

POM'CANNELLE

RESTAURANT
SALON DE THE
PATISSERIES
GLACES

DEGUSTATION
DE GLACES
ET SORBETS
DE LA MAISON
BERTHILLON

CHOCOLATS

ABOVE A patisserie window with an abundance of interesting gâteaux.

RIGHT The French are a nation of chocolate lovers. Facchetti – chocolatiers.

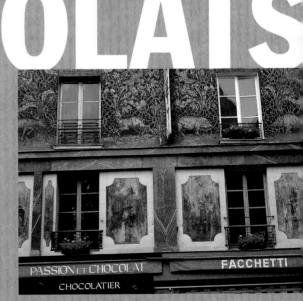

PASSION ET CHOCOLAT
CHOCOLATIER

FACCHETTI

purchase. Probably the most famous *fromagerie* is Androuet, in the Rue d'Amsterdam. There the cheeses are matured on the premises and they stock about 200 different types at any one time. Buying cheese in France is a very different experience from buying cheese anywhere else in the world. When you compare these beautiful, fat, yellow Bries made from raw milk to the hard, pale chalky ones we often find elsewhere, you can hardly believe you are eating the same thing. Lillo in the Rue des Belles-Feuilles, specialises in cooked cheese and sells delicious filled crepes and elegant tarts as well as unpasteurised cream and milk.

Paris is home to many beautiful brasseries many of which have interesting histories. Technically a brasserie is just a place where simply prepared dishes are served and drinks are available, but several examples in Paris far exceed this description. In 1968 an Alsatian named Jean-Paul Bucher bought the Brasserie Flo (metro Chateau d'Eau) which became a huge success and is now the flagship of his restaurant empire. It was built in 1886 and is all polished wood and gleaming brass rails and moleskin benches. Everyday people flock there to enjoy the excellent seafood and hearty sauerkraut that is typical of the Flo group's menus.

La Coupole, an enormous art deco brasserie, was built in the 1920s and attracted famous thinkers, painters and writers such as Lenin, Picasso, Aragon, Man Ray and Scott Fitzgerald. Acquired by Jean-Paul Bucher in 1987, Parisians were aghast when he announced that it was closing for renovation. However, when it reopened in 1989 the paintings, the 33 columns in the room and

LEFT A fish market displaying a variety of freshly caught fish.

RIGHT Recently restored to its former glory, La Coupole restaurant in its early days.

everything else had been beautifully restored, and it is now as beautiful as ever. Julien's interior is a near perfect example of art nouveau and has a famous Cuban mahogany bar designed by Louis Majorelle. Its situation in the Rue du Faubourg Saint-Denis makes it one of the best places to go for a late supper after the theatre.

INTERNATIONAL CUISINE

Paris is an international city and this is reflected in the hundreds of restaurants which are not French. An aftermath of French colonialism, there are a great many North African restaurants, serving marvellous couscous, tagines and grilled meat. Chez Omar, in the Rue de Bretagne, is a very well known spot and is always busy, and Oum el Banine, in the Rue Dufrenoy, near the Bois de Boulogne provides Moroccan food with an innovative style. There are also some black African restaurants, often located in the less expensive neighbourhoods.

There are many more Vietnamese and Cambodian restaurants in Paris than there are Chinese, again for historical reasons. The Tan Dinh in the Rue de Verneuil is a Vietnamese place run by two brothers who are Vietnamese nouvelle cuisine enthusiasts and, unusually, they keep a notable cellar.

RIGHT Kosher food shops cater to the Jewish community.

ABOVE Nam Phuong – A Chinese and Vietnamese restaurant.

RIGHT A patisserie and salon de thé supplying oriental delicacies.

ABOVE The canopy of the world-famous Maxim's restaurant.

RIGHT The amazing roof café at the Musée D'Orsay.

Belleville, in the 11th *arrondissement,* is fast becoming the new Chinatown (or South-East Asia town) of Paris, complete with noodle bars and Oriental supermarkets. In comparison to London, Indian restaurants are few and far between. Those that succeed are often rather posh and pricey – not the sort of place you would just fall into after a movie with tandoori chicken on your mind.

If you want to though, and take the trouble to do a little research, you can eat almost anything you can think of in this city. It is the combination of the variety and availability of first class ingredients, classic and simple French food and multi-cultural cuisines that makes Paris such a memorable eating experience and is one of the main reasons that it is said that Paris belongs not just to the French, but to the world.

ABOVE Street cafés at the Place des Vosges.

LEFT Les Deux Magots, a pavement café in St Germain-des-Prés.

Text: Paul Roland

Jane Birkin and Serge Gainsbourg in 1971 – their 1967
'heavy breathing' hit 'Je t'aime, Moi Non Plus' wowed
record buyers (and censors) with its French explicitness.

As early as the Middle Ages the creative life of France has been centralised in Paris to which the country's most historically important and culturally influential composers and musicians have felt irresistibly drawn.

Parisians have always frowned upon provincialism, an attitude which has encouraged its artists to enshrine national sensibilities in music which has been in defiance of international trends. When composers such as Lully, Gluck and Stravinsky were adopted by the city they were expected to embrace the French attitude to almost everything, including a certain characteristic conservatism. They did so readily, and usually with a passion. Consequently the music of Paris has a continuity and character quite unlike that of any other European city, although it has certainly been subject to its own stylistic revolutions.

THE MIDDLE AGES TO BAROQUE

The musical life of Paris could be said to have begun with the completion of Notre Dame in the 1180s when the cathedral became a focus for the development of medieval church music throughout Europe. Until that time religious music was limited to devotional plainsong which, as the name implies, was confined to a simple melodic line sung in unison without harmony or measured rhythm. Composers such as Leonin and his successor Perotin established what amounted to a school for writers of sacred vocal music within the cathedral, adding complementary melodic lines to create polyphony and by so doing develop the motet (a sacred song for three voices).

Outside the capital the troubadours and their contemporaries, the trouveres (originators of the modern French language), were bringing songs of courtly love to provincial courts and noble houses, making France the most significant cultural centre in Europe during the Middle Ages.

The first efforts to devise a system of musical notation originated a century later in Notre Dame in response to the increasing complexity of church music. At the same time secular songs were becoming less formularised and more rhythmically intricate contributing to a period of prolific creativity later dubbed Ars Nova (New Art).

By the early 16th century Paris had become a centre for a new form, the chanson, an early form of popular song for solo voice and lute. Instrumental versions of the most popular pieces by Janequin, Certon and Sermisy formed the basic repertoire of all dance music performed throughout Europe for almost a century afterwards, contributing to the city becoming one of two major centres for music publishing and the manufacture of musical instruments (the other being Lyon).

Secular music gained further respectability among the sophisticates with the founding of Baif's Académie de Poésie et de Musique in Paris in 1570. Here the composers were encouraged to write music for verse in the classical Greek style, creating an art form which anticipated the birth of Italian opera by at least half a century.

ABOVE An illustration from a 16th Century book of royal songs entitled *Chants Royaux sur la Conception Couronnée du Puy de Rouan*, showing a choir conducted by Jean Ockeghem.

LEFT Pages of music for the nativity for the organist Frangois de Layelle, printed in Lyon by Guaynard in 1528.

F. chauveau del. L. louette fecit.

ATYS

THE BIRTH OF OPERA

Opera itself was slow in coming to France, partly because Parisians preferred drama and ballet and it was they who dictated the nation's taste. Ballet as a professional entertainment was born in Paris, and the French ballets of the 17th century were heavily interspersed with vocal highlights. They also boasted extravagant scenery and theatrical effects which evidently satisfied the audience's appetite for music and drama under one roof.

It was not until 1669 that the first French opera company, the Académie de Musique (more commonly known as the Paris Opera), was founded to 'sing plays in company'. Its first creative head was the Italian born composer Jean Baptiste Lully (1632-1687) who dominated French opera until his death by virtue of a royal patent which prevented competition. His 13 *tragédies lyriques*, written in his adopted French with ballet interludes and much spectacle, proved popular with both the public (who sang them in the streets of Paris) and his royal patron Louis XIV, but effectively isolated French opera from the vital Italian influence.

Although his influence proved pervasive and rather stifling for his fellow composers Lully single-handedly defined French music during the Baroque era and was responsible for developing the formal French overture. He also modernised violin-bowing technique and was one of the first composers to use a large staff as a baton. Unfortunately, in his enthusiasm during a performance to celebrate the king's recovery from an illness, he injured himself with his staff and died soon after of blood poisoning.

When Louis XIV withdrew from public functions due to ill-health the popularity of opera declined until Jean Philippe Rameau (1683-1764) revitalised the form in the second half of the 18th century. Rameau emphasised the Gallic penchant for music of refinement and elegance and he was largely responsible for the creation of a new, essentially French form of opera – *opéra-comique* – after a fierce debate (known as Guerre des Bouffons) divided the champions of French music against those who saw Italian

ABOVE Jean Baptiste Lully, the architect of French opera in the Baroque era.

BELOW Orchestrating the 18th Century French opera revival Jean Phillippe Rameau.

as the true language of opera. Despite its name, *opéra-comique* was not always light and amusing. It was a term intended rather to indicate the inclusion of some element of spoken dialogue in the work, to distinguish it from the 'serious' opera which linked arias with accompanied recitative.

CULTURAL RENAISSANCE AND REVOLUTION

In the years leading up to the Revolution in 1789 Paris was particularly rich in music making with a number of celebrated concert series being established to promote the city as the cultural centre of Europe.

The Concert Spirituel, which was set up to provide orchestral performances during the religious holidays when the opera was closed, commissioned the twenty-two-year-old Mozart to write a symphony in celebration of the capital. The 'Paris Symphony' was actually written during Mozart's stay in the city in 1778, although he left it untitled and afterward replaced the slow movement. Another cultural institution, Concerts de la Loge Olympia, commissioned Haydn's set of six 'Paris Symphonies' which were performed for the first time in 1780.

Another eminent and influential figure of the classical period, Christoph Willibald Gluck (1714-1787), the great opera reformer, was also drawn to the French capital where he felt the cultural climate would be conducive to his passionate crusade for realism.

Indeed, in the latter years of his life the city of Paris was to inspire him to produce several key works which re-established the focal role of the orchestra, trimming some of the excesses that had been imposed on composers up until that point by self-indulgent prima donnas.

During the Revolution the opera houses of Paris remained open and their repertoire was largely unaffected by events, but public concerts were devoted almost exclusively to martial music, while sacred music was all but drowned out by 'politically correct' hymns to Liberty, such as Gossec's Requiem for the Martyrs of the Revolution.

Gossec, who was a former director of Concert Spirituel, was a founding figure of the Paris Conservatory which had been established in 1795 to ensure that the state controlled and directed tuition in all the major musical institutions.

ABOVE A costume for a demon in the Lully opera *Armide*, which was also used in a production of *Psyche* by the English composer Matthew Locke.

RIGHT An illustration for the music manuscript cover of Berlioz's opera *The Damnation of Faust*, written in 1846.

MUSIC OF THE FIRST AND SECOND EMPIRE

Napoleon's reign encouraged the return of
lyric tragedies with their heroic themes and
spectacle, although the *opéra-comique*
continued to prove popular because of its
exclusively French-language repertoire.

When the monarchy was restored in
1815 Paris found itself the focal point of
the operatic world due in part to the heavy
subsidies which Napoleon had lavished upon
the national opera house. Its vast wealth
helped the company to stage the fashionable
and spectacular Grande Operas of the day,
and to hire the services of some of Europe's
most celebrated composers, most notably
Rossini (who wrote *Guillaume Tell* especially
for Paris) and Meyerbeer.

But this success helped create something
of a clique among those who controlled the
musical life of Paris and its institutions, an
exclusivity which ironically alienated one of
the most characteristic French composers of
the classical period, Hector Berlioz (1803-
1869). In response Berlioz augmented his
income from music by writing stinging and
incisive critiques of Parisian musical life.
These endeared him to European audiences
where his works enjoyed great popularity, but
further distanced him from his countrymen
and ensured that he remained largely
unrecognised in his own country.

In this insular environment it fell to
private individuals and philanthropists
among the bankers, nobility and even the
piano manufacturers of Paris to assume the
role of patrons of the arts.

But while they championed the music
of the so-called moderns such as Liszt (who
found fame there as a young virtuoso pianist
before becoming a composer) and Chopin
(who died in Paris in 1849), conservatism
stubbornly persisted in the corridors of the
capital's artistic institutions. Even after the
1848 revolution Verdi incorporated ballet
into his one French-language opera *Don
Carlos* to please the Parisian audiences, as did
Wagner when reviving *Tannhauser* for the
Paris Opera in 1860.

The continual stream of émigré composers
continued nevertheless, each charmed by the
warmth of their host's embrace. On his arrival
in Paris in September 1831 Chopin, a
fastidious dresser, had described the city in a
letter to a friend. 'One finds here in Paris

magnificent riches, filthy streets, the most virtuous people and the most depraved', he wrote. 'One may dress like a derelict and still be accepted by the best society.'

In 1875 the present Paris Opera house, designed by Charles Garnier, was opened with a seating capacity of 2,600 and boasting a stage 30 metres wide and 34 metres deep. On viewing the ornate interior one critic commented, 'Inside – and this is where the Opera has it over the interior-less Albert Memorial – the building is decorated with the same abandoned fantaisie and orgiastic delight in banal extravagance for its own sake. Only more so.'

Even with the prospect of such an opulent setting new French composers of the post-revolutionary period such as Gounod (1818-1893) and Bizet (1838-1875), both Parisian born, turned to the recently established Théâtre Lyrique (est. 1851) in the hope of having their operas produced. However, Parisians in the Second Empire preferred the light and frothy operettas of Offenbach at the new Théâtre des Bouffes-Parisiens.

BELOW The magnificent Paris Opera, here seen in a photograph taken in the early 20th Century.

ABOVE A portrait of the opera diva Celestine Galli-Marie in her 1905 title role of Bizet's *Carmen*.

THE IMPRESSIONISTS

The latter years of the 19th century saw the awakening of a new national identity stimulated by the nation's defeat at the hands of the Prussians and the traumatic siege of Paris in 1870. In response a group of young French composers led by Saint-Saëns, Fauré and Massenet founded the Société Nationale de Musique with the intention of encouraging new composers to storm the ramparts of the cultural consciousness, but they made little impact on a firmly entrenched establishment.

It was not until 1889 that French music finally found a unique and readily identifiable voice in the atmospheric collages of sound commonly known as Impressionism. The movement began in a single surge of inspiration during a visit to the Paris Exposition Universelle by the then twenty-seven-year-old Claude Debussy (1862-1918). The Parisian born composer was inspired by a performance by Javanese gamelan bands into creating an entirely new form of music for the coming century, music of an emotional ambiguity. Of the Javanese he later commented, 'Their Conservatoire is the rhythm of the sea, the wind rustling the leaves and the myriad sounds of nature.'

His contemporary, Maurice Ravel (1875-1937), yet another graduate of the Paris Conservatory, made music which was far more French in terms of temperament and with the consummate care of a craftsman, prompting Stravinsky to compare him to a Swiss watchmaker.

But the mantle of maestro of the modern movement must reside with Stravinsky himself whose overnight fame was ignited with the Parisian premiere of his ballet *The Firebird* in 1910 produced by the Svengali of revolutionary Russian ballet, Serge Diaghilev. Three years later the composer's *Rite of Spring* sparked riots in the Champs Elysées Theatre and fierce partisan debate among the city's critics and intellectuals.

Curiously, the controversy only served to enhance the reputation of the new generation of Parisian composers such as Ravel, Debussy, Satie, Poulenc, Auric and Milhaud who had each aligned themselves with Diaghilev in the wake of Stravinsky's critical and popular success, and provided the Ballets Russe with new scores.

TOP Claude Debussy in front of his house in the Avenue du Bois in 1910.

ABOVE A portrait of Maurice Ravel at work, circa 1930.

STRAVINSKY

ABOVE Tamara Karasavina, ballerina with Diaghilev's celebrated Ballets Russes, as she appeared in Igor Stravinsky's *Firebird* in Paris in 1911.

LEFT Igor Stravinsky photographed in 1937.

ABOVE An illustration by
Paul Colin for a poster
advertising Josephine Baker
at the Champs-Elysées
Music Hall in 1925.

After the First World War Paris became a centre for study rather than innovation in classical music, attracting international composers such as Aaron Copland to the Conservatory, while Parisian composers such as Milhaud looked to America to absorb the new jazz idioms.

The rise of the avant-garde, led by Olivier Messiaen (1908-1992), during the inter-war years, was stifled by the Nazi occupation, but after the Liberation Paris once again became a centre for new music, attracting modernists such as Boulez and Stockhausen to courses conducted by Messiaen.

JAZZIN' AT THE HOT CLUB

During the inter-war years the focus shifted away from so called 'serious music' to popular street songs and American jazz, although Parisians often preferred their jazz sweet and light, soufflé style.

France's first taste of the new form had come in 1902 when a review, *Joyeux Negres*, opened at the Nouveau Cirque in Paris, shocking the sensibilities of cafe society and captivating leading classical composers such as Claude Debussy and Erik Satie, and delighting intellectuals like Jean Cocteau.

By the 1920s both American and home-grown jazz bands were a regular attraction at concert halls, cabarets and night clubs, such as the famous Boeuf-sur-le-toit (the first jazz club in Europe), Ben Benjamin's Blue Note Club near the Champs-Elysées and the Club St Germain on the Left Bank, while the exotic dancer and comedienne from New York's Harlem, Josephine Baker, introduced a taste of the music to the customers at the Champs-Elysées Music Hall and the Casino de Paris before taking up residency at the Folies Bergere.

Although jazz was an American idiom European jazz found eloquent expression in the Paris based Quintette du Hot Club de France founded in 1934 by Belgian born gypsy guitarist Django Reinhardt (1910-1953) and the violin virtuoso Stephane Grappelli (b.1908).

Reinhardt, who had lost the use of three fingers on his left hand in a fire, developed a unique style which could be described as refined melancholia leading to him becoming the first European musician to have a lasting influence on American jazz players, guitarists

BELOW From around 1931, complete with pet leopard the great black American entertainer who made Paris her own, Josephine Baker.

BOTTOM An advertisement from a 1941 music magazine for Django Reinhardt material on the Disques Swing label.

SWING
DJANGO REINHARDT

ABOVE The legendary American tenor saxophone player Coleman Hawkins who was an ardent admirer of Django Reinhardt.

BELOW Maurice Chevalier on the front of sheet music for 'Avec le Sourire' (left) and a 1938 *Paris Match*.

in particular. When Paris became an obligatory stop-over for touring jazz bands during the 1930s Django was invited to play with all the legendary American soloists of the period including the saxophone giants Coleman Hawkins and Benny Carter.

His Parisian-born partner Stephane Grappelli made his reputation with the Hot Club by adapting the violin to jazz, rather than diluting the music to suit the instrument.

After the Hot Club's demise with Reinhardt's death, Grappelli became a regular feature on the international concert and club circuit in the 1960s and 70s and found himself one of the most popular jazz violinists in the music's history and one of the few to have made the 'crossover' with credibility and conviction. His violin 'duels' with Yehudi Menuhin, and fellow Frenchmen Jean Luc Ponty and Didier Lockwood, have ensured that the distinctive Gallic flavour of French jazz has been carried beyond the boundaries of France and Europe.

CABARET AND CHANSON

Chic and charming are the two adjectives which most readily come to mind when describing the French popular songs of the pre-rock era, from the 1920s to the 1950s.

Singers such as Edith Piaf, Maurice Chevalier, Charles Trenet and Jean Sablon emerged from the twilight world of the

Parisian music-hall, night club and dance-hall, or 'bal', to become international stars, despite the fact that many of their songs were often in very colloquial and argotic French.

These chanson and cabaret singers were at once uniquely French and at the same time universally appealing with their cheerfully fatalistic songs of doomed romance and elegant despair.

Maurice Chevalier personified the sophisticated, carefree spirit that many identified with Paris, the City of Lights, while one-time street singer Edith Piaf (1915-1963) expressed its shadow side in songs a French critic dubbed 'The Folklore of the Future'. During the war years Piaf (whose name is Parisian argot for 'sparrow') was the most popular singer in France, her husky, soul-baring style expressing the suppressed emotions of a nation under siege.

Other 'singers of charm', as they were called, included Charles Aznavour, who began his career at the Comédie-Française during the German occupation, and Georges

ABOVE The 'little sparrow' Edith Piaf, at the Paris Olympia in 1962.

BELOW Charles Aznavour poses in front of the Sacré-Coeur in Montmartre.

Ulmer, a Dane who settled in Paris after World War Two and immortalised the Pigalle, its bistros and its exotic nightlife in the song of the same name.

PARISIAN POP

The frantic urban sound of rock'n'roll was unleashed on French adolescents largely through the European-based AFN radio station (American Forces Network) in the late Fifties, and had the same galvanising impact on the nation's youth as it did elsewhere. However, with typical Gallic humour the French imitators dubbed it 'yaourt' (yoghurt) in an attempt to imitate the hillbilly hiccup pioneered by Elvis Presley which came to characterise many of the early rock records.

The first club devoted to rock concerts appeared in Paris in 1959, namely the Golf Drouot on the corner of the Boulevard Montmarte and Rue Drouot. Before long Paris was the setting for the first French rock festival at the Palais des Sports in 1961, the main attraction being the immensely popular (in his native land) and seemingly immortal Johnny Hallyday, who was once flamboyantly described as 'Elvis Presley and Cliff Richard rolled into one'.

LEFT An institution in his native France, and resident in St Tropez for many years, Johnny Hallyday.

RIGHT Another Sixties icon of French popular music, the enigmatic singer and songwriter Françoise Hardy.

JACQUES BRE

But the French preference for singers with poetic lyrics – and the emotional and vocal range to carry them convincingly – meant that the beat groups of the Sixties as often as not lost out to singer-songwriters such as Françoise Hardy and her one-time boyfriend Jacques Dutronc.

One of the most influential and internationally successful singer-songwriters of the post-war period was the Belgian born Jacques Brel who served his apprenticeship singing in Paris cafes before becoming one of the leading French romantic singers of the modern era.

Once regarded as the poor provincial cousin of 'the real thing', releasing occasional novelty hits such as the sexually titillating and much-banned 'Je t'aime, Moi Non Plus' (recorded in 1969 by British actress Jane Birkin and French vocalist-songwriter Serge Gainsbourg) and 'Joe le Taxi' (sung by Vanessa Paradis), French pop music has now acquired a cult ambience and (albeit often kitsch) collectability.

In recent years British bands such as Suede, Saint Etienne and Blur have each covered French pop songs of the Sixties (the latter with Françoise Hardy), while the Gallic spirit continues uncompromisingly in the Parisian bands Dimitri, Air, and the aptly named Daft Punk.

ABOVE Straight out of the Bardot 'child-woman' mould, the contemporary singer Vanessa Paradis.

RIGHT A name in 'indie' circles far beyond their native shores, the anarchic Paris rock band Daft Punk.

SPORTS

Paris seems to have a history of generating sporti
ideas. From FIFA the international body ruling foot
to the World Cup itself. It has hosted the Olympic
Games, the Tour de France and many Tennis event

Text: Brian Glanville

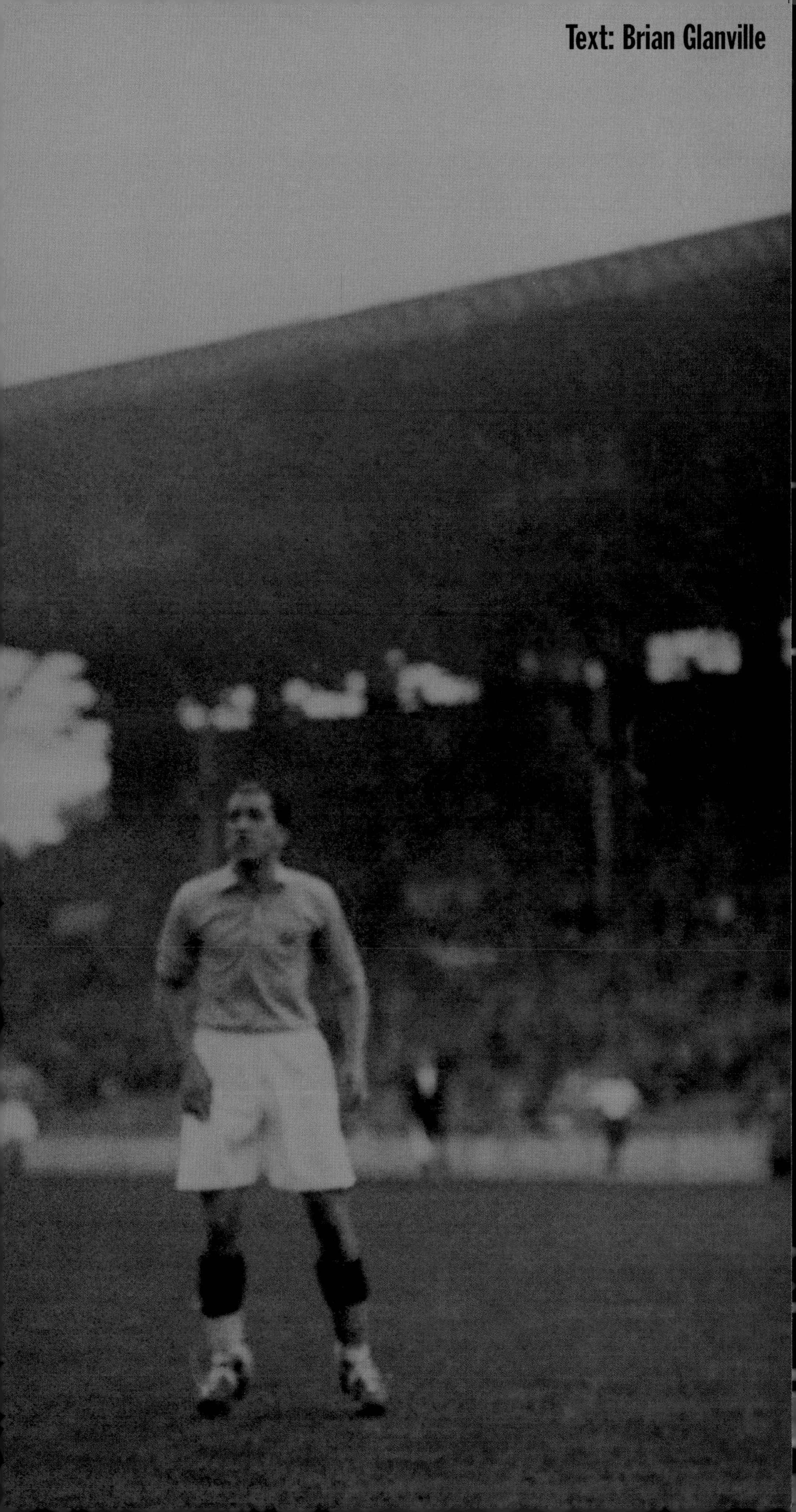

Round about the quarter final stage of the 1998 World Cup, Didier Deschamps, the captain of the French international team, publicly bewailed the lack of passion among the spectators at the Stade Français in Saint Denis when France played. Too many of them, he bewailed, came in their suits and ties. What he wanted plainly was the 'real' fans, the working class supporters who would usually pack the Parc des Princes – still used for the World Cup, but largely superseded – the 'tieless' ones who would cheer their team to the end.

LE SPORT

In the event, passions and enthusiasm mounted. After the semi final, when the French prevailed against Croatia, there was joy and celebration in the streets of Paris, a kind of peaceful 1968. After the final, congestion, confusion, ecstasy. Cars which tried to get through the mob had a futile task. Two drivers in fact were arrested after they had ploughed into the unlucky celebrants.

All this might symptomise the strange ambivalence of Paris to sport in general. As a 'sporting' city, its credentials are formidable. It has twice staged the World Cup finals at 60 years' remove, twice put on the Olympic games – on a smaller scale in 1900, and then whole-heartedly 24 years later, the Games recalled in the film *Chariots Of Fire,* when the English sprinter, Harold Abrahams – a Cambridge blue – won the 100 metres, and a dazzling Uruguayan side won the soccer tournament.

Paris seems to generate sporting ideas. FIFA, the international body which rules football, was conceived there early this century, when the French were virtually learning to play. 'The Frenchmen did not play football, they frivolled,' wrote the facetious *Football Chat,* when France sent not one but two teams to the Olympic tournament at White City, both of which were thrashed, with players who outraged convention by smoking at half time.

It was the French, notably the late Gabriel Hanot, by turns player, administrator and journalist, who conceived the European Champion's Cup, initiated in 1955. And it was the Frenchman, Jules Rimet, who was chiefly responsible for the birth of the World Cup itself.

And yet. . .Paris at present has a vigorously effective, very well supported team in Paris Saint Germain which, despite the birth of the larger, far more modern, stadium at Saint Denis insists on remaining at the Parc des Princes. Yet Paris S-G, as they are popularly known, rose from the ashes of so many other Parisian clubs. There was Matra Racing, sponsored by the wealthy, powerful Matra company, which spent a lot of money, bought a lot of stars, then suddenly and embarrassingly collapsed, leaving Paris S-G, founded in 1973, to pick up the pieces of Parisian soccer, Racing Club de Paris, The Penguins, in their famous blue and white

hoops, were the aristocrats of French football, playing a much cherished game each Armistice Day against London's Arsenal.

Yet by 1966 support in Paris was so pathetically low that Racing were obliged, humiliatingly and absurdly, to throw in their lot with distant, modest Sedan, a further absurdity – and a deeply self-defeating one – being the arrangement that alternative fixtures were played in Sedan and Paris. Needless to say it did not last very long, Racing virtually disappeared as a professional club, having a kind of ghostly resurrection under the aegis of Matra.

But they are not the only Parisian club either to fall on evil times or to disappear completely. What of Red Star, CAP and Stade Français, all of whom had their days of glory, before disappearing into the vast void of Parisian indifference? In vain did Bernard Louis Lavy strike to keep Racing Club afloat. Not till the arrival of the lively if sometimes controversial Francis Borelli did Paris Saint Germain at last bring professional football successfully back to fickle Paris. 'Paris is worth a mass,' said Henry IV of Navarre. But you sometimes wondered whether it was worth a football club.

COUPE DU MONDE 1938

LEFT Monsieur Jules Rimet meets the players of the Amateur Football Championship, 1930s.

ABOVE The Italian and Hungarian captains shake hands before the World Cup Final, Paris 1938.

ABOVE A promotion for the same model bicycle as ridden by the great Garin in the Paris-Brest-Paris race.

RIGHT Tour de France cyclists plus hangers-on and pressmen passing under the Arc de Triomphe into the Champs-Elysée.

BELOW Garin is also featured on the cover of this 1903 publication *The Outdoor Life* celebrating the Tour de France.

TOUR DE FRANCE

Also invented in Paris was the Tour de France which, having survived for most of the century, seemed to have possibly breathed its last in 1998, when it was shown to disastrous effect, that many of the teams were taking drugs. Cyclists in such gruelling races have been taking drugs for many years. (One of the best English cyclists of all time, Tommy Simpson, actually died in the Tour de France as a consequence.) But although drug use has become seemingly endemic, the affection of the French public for the race, the drama and the spectacle as the cyclists sweep majestically into Paris for the last lap, ensures the grand Tour has yet to pass the point of no return.

The national Olympic games of 1900 coincided with the Paris International Exhibition. There were such strange oddities as an underwater swimming race and obstacle race, not to mention a tug of war – in which a combined Danish-Swedish team defeated the United States. The athletics programmes was haphazard. Under the heading of République Française, Exposition Universelle de 1900, they were mildly farcical. The setting for the two day event was the Bois de Boulogne, where a 500 metre grass track had been laid, and at certain points, competitors disappeared into the trees! Not only was the turf thick; it was abundantly watered. Both the sprint course and the run up for the long jump were allegedly downhill.

VIII OLYMPIADE

· JEVX OLYMPIQVES

· PARIS 1924·

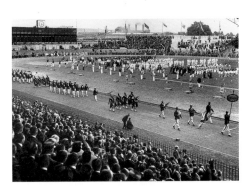

ABOVE The Opening Day of the 1924 Summer Olympics, Paris.

LEFT One of the many posters advertising the Olympic Games.

BELOW US Olympic Gold medalist, also of *Tarzan* fame, Johnny Weissmuller,

This did not stop the formidably versatile American Alvin Kraenzlein of Pennsylvania winning the 60 metres sprint, two hurdles titles and the long jump. Americans indeed dominated the athletics, taking no fewer than 17 of the titles. France took just one; the marathon, through Michel Theato. Britain did rather better, with four victories.

1924 was a much more serious affair. Dominated as always by the athletics, it also featured not only a soccer tournament with 23 teams but a 23 team Rugby tournament, in which the USA beat France 17-3. Since those remote days, French Rugby, of course, has become a major international force, with many a dramatic game in Paris, even though the city has never really been a major player in the sport.

Swimming in an open air pool was especially impressive, notable for the achievements of America's Johnny Weissmuller, later to become the most famous cinematic Tarzan of the Apes, and the redoubtable 33 year old Duke Kahanamakou, competing in his 3rd Olympic games and winning another silver medal. Johnny Weissmuller, who beat Duke into second place, in the 100 metres, also annexed the 400 and the 4 X 200 metres freestyle. The margin of his victory over Duke Kahanamakou was a yawning 2.4 seconds. Duke had won that race in 1912 and 1920.

France won gold medals only in the cycling, fencing and gymnastics. The USA won a dozen medals in the athletics, but Britain took not only the 100 meters through Harold Abrahams but the 400 metres with Eric Liddell – who might have beaten Abrahams had he been prepared as a good Christian to run on a Sunday – and the 800 metres through Douglas Lowe.

In soccer, virtually a professional affair, Uruguay annihilated the Swiss 3-0 in the Final with a team which included such stars as Joss Andrade in defence and Hector Scarone in attack.

ABOVE Harold Abrahams runs and wins the Olympic 100 metres.

OPPOSITE Eric Liddell's victory win of the Gold medal in the 400 metres.

GRAND SLAM

Paris is of course also a notable centre of tennis. Between the wars, France with the so-called Four Musketeers, Cochet, Borotra, Lacoste and Brugon, dominated the international Davis Cup for years. Jean Borotra, nicknamed The Bounding Basque, might not have had the technique of Henri Cochet, but his energy was enormous, having been taught the game when on summer holidays in England. Today, the hard courts tournament at the Stade Roland Garros is an important stage of the so-called Grand Slam, where financial rewards have risen massively over the years. These are courts which can undo the finest of grass court Titans, as Pete Sampras, who went on to win yet another Wimbledon in 1998, previously found to his

LIDDELL

BOROTRA
BRUGON
LACOSTE
COCHET

ABOVE Playing at Roland Garros, 1928.

RIGHT France's 'Four Musketeers'.

cost. He went out embarrassingly early at Roland Garros, where the big serve and volley game is not at a premium.

Paris in the 1920s had a notable heroine in Suzanne Lenglen, the brilliant French girl who for four years dominated tennis, seen as a potential star when she was a mere 13. Her demanding father had coached her, making her practice endlessly. Essentially a hard courts player, she astonished Wimbledon by winning at her first attempt. At a time when women's tennis was something of a poor relation, such was the interest in her that the organizers, despite themselves were forced to put the Final of the women's event on the Centre Court.

In the Davis Cup, France had an astonishing run, though it was facilitated by the convention of the so called Challenge Round, which bizarrely allowed the holders a bye (missing a round) all the way to the Final! So it was that France, having defeated the USA in 1927, after two consecutive defeats, were able to play the next half a dozen finals in Paris, winning five of them before succumbing to Britain and the irresistible Fred Perry in 1933. After which the French hegemony was at an end.

ABOVE RIGHT 'Miss Lenglen, Champion of the world of lawn tennis' on a magazine cover, 1919.

RIGHT The champion in action at one of her many successful matches.

année. — N° 206.   LE N° : 60 CENT. (TOUS LES VENDREDIS)

J'ai vu

MLLE LENGLEN ET... SON OMBRE

La joueuse, qui va représenter la France aux matches internationaux, reprend ici une ba...

The Tour de France was the concept of a famous cyclist, Henri Desgrange, who had set the initial world record for the hour. Editor, in Paris, of a sports newspaper called *L'Auto,* later to become *L'Equipe,* which would continue to sponsor the great race with *Le Parisien Libéré,* Desgrange initiated the Tour in 1903. It then covered 1510 miles in six massive stages. He invented the bestowing of the Yellow Jersey on whatever rider won the current stage, the colour being chosen because it was that of the pages of *L'Auto.* That first race was somewhat blemished by the fact that not all the riders rode all the stages. One of them indeed, suffering from cramp, travelled a stage by train. The capable winner was Maurice Garin, a naturalized Italian, by profession a chimney-sweep. He also won another famous race three times – the Paris Roubaix. His tour-winning margin was a vast 2 hours and 49 minutes.

After only the second Tour an overwhelmed Desgrange proclaimed that it would have to be the last one, 'because it had been killed by its success, by the uncontrollable passions it had released'. It survived to become an institution.

WORLD CUP

As for soccer, the first FIFA meeting was held in Paris on May 21, 1904. Significantly, the six European countries involved added in the constitutional document a proviso that FIFA alone could organize a world championship. In 26 years the dream became reality.

Two men nurtured the dream and inspired the development of French soccer: Jules

LEFT Suzanne Lenglen – appeared on magazine covers everywhere.

RIGHT Winner of the Tour de France in 1951 – Swiss Hugo Koblet.

ABOVE Michel Platini gets up above the Spain defence in the European Championship in Paris, 1984.

Rimet, after whom the World Cup would initially be named, and Henri Delauney, Secretary of the French Football Federation from 1908 to 1956.

In 1938, the French put on the third World Cup. By then their own football had long been up and running. As early as 1921 their amateur team had been good enough to beat the English amateurs 2-1 in Paris. Ten years later, again in Paris, France thrashed the full England team 5-2. In 1938, the prospect of war loomed over a tournament which lost two major contestants. Spain was locked in civil war; Austria, swallowed in the Anschluss by Germany, was obliged to provide players for a so called Greater German team.

The 1998 World Cup began somewhat inauspiciously in Paris with a parade through the centre of giant animated figures, a source of amusement rather than admiration. Initially, there was no great optimism or even, it seemed enthusiasm in France for their team, notorious for its inability to score goals. The usual rent-a-quote psychologists were called up to explain this seeming indifference; one of them suggested it was based on pessimism, itself induced by France's lack of International success in recent years, though they had won the European Championship in 1984, beating Spain, in Paris in the Final.

The rebuilt Parc des Princes had survived some severe early problems. The pitch itself had long been spoilt by those who played on it and one night (thank goodness it was at night) the roof of one of the stands had collapsed. Several games, including the Third Place match, would take place in the Parc des Princes, which had recently staged the all Italian UEFA Cup Final in which Inter beat Lazio. But it was the stadium at Saint Denis, erected at colossal expense, which would take priority.

France would play their last three games at Saint Denis. Against Italy, at least the crowd sang the Marseillaise with some emotion, though the passion was still in abeyance. In the end the French prevailed on penalties after extra time against an over-cautious Italy, then Thuram's goals conquered Croatia.

Brazil were strong favourites for the Final but the Brazilian team didn't even warm up; crashing 3-0. Zinedine Zidane headed 2 goals from corners. And there was joy in the streets, not least in a packed Champs-Elysées.

BELOW French manager, Aime Jaquet holds up the victory cup after the World Cup Final against Brazil, 1998.

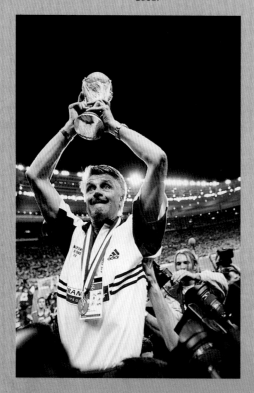

BELOW Zidane scores the first goal of the game – France v. Brazil at the Stade De France.

BOTTOM Celebration on the streets of Paris – the Champs-Elysées after the French victory.

ZIDANE

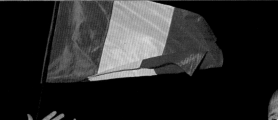

Text: Stephanie Driver

The French farce, which reached its peak in the work of
playwrite Georges Feydeau – as in this scene from his
Un Fil à la Patte – is just one of the traditions that has
contributed to making the Paris stage truly unique.

STAGE & F

Home of the Moulin Rouge and the Comédie-Française, La Nouvelle Vague and Molière, Paris is artistically a city of contrast. Perhaps no other city in the world combines its reverence for classic traditions with such a rigorous search for the shocking and the innovative. The result is an exciting mix of film and theatre arts that resonates around the world. With great publicly-funded theatre companies, thriving commercial boulevard theatres, numerous independent cinemas and an internationally renowned cabaret scene (as well as international ballet and opera), Paris is as culturally alive today as it ever has been. Its diversity stands as a testimony to its population's belief that the performing arts stand at the centre of public life – a belief that goes back to the beginnings of the Parisian theatre.

LE THEATR

LEFT A painting by Jean Beraud of the street scene at the front entrance to the Théâtre du Vaudeville.

ABOVE The Cirque d'Hiver, here staging a musical based on the life and songs of Edith Piaf.

BELOW RIGHT The Théâtre des Varietes in an engraving by Lowry from a drawing by J. Nash.

THE BIRTH OF PARIS THEATRE

Medieval Miracle and Mystère (mystery) plays were entertaining the people of the city as early as the 12th Century. During the main church festivals, performances of religious plays were acted by members of the town guilds, usually on the back of carts or on improvised stages. Often these popular religious plays were mixed with secular farces, presented by roaming bands of young comics known as Sociétés Joyeuses. By the 15th Century, these part-time actors had formed their own guild of amateur players. Known as the Confrérie de la Passion, they held a monopoly over all the acting in Paris for the next 200 years.

It wasn't until 1578, by which time the performance of religious plays had become illegal, that the first fully professional theatre company appeared in Paris. The Comédiens du Roi had made their name in the provinces. Now, they leased a venue from the Confrérie de la Passion and made their home in Paris at the Hôtel de Bourgogne.

With the Confrérie's monopoly broken, the Hôtel de Bourgogne soon had a serious rival in the Théâtre du Marais. It was here, under the leadership of the actor Guillaume Montdory, that the first performance of a new play by the young playwright, Pierre Corneille, took place in 1637. Because it did not adhere to the classical principals of playwrighting – particularly the demand for all the action to take place in real time and in

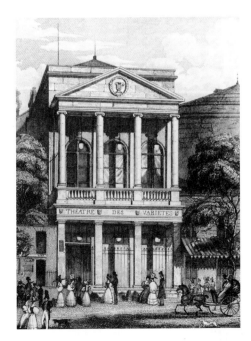

ABOVE Théâtre Française, the original home of the Comédie-Française.

one location – *Le Cid* caused a sensation.

The tragedies of Corneille, and later, his rival Racine, author of such dramas as *Phèdre* and *Andromaque*, belong to a period that became known as *le grand siècle* (the great century). Both authors' works have been frequently revived over the centuries. However, despite their lasting renown, the defining figure of the period was another man: Jean-Baptiste Poquelin – better known to the world as Molière.

MOLIÈRE

Jean-Baptiste Poquelin was born in Paris in 1622. The son of a successful merchant who held a minor position at court, by 1643 he had abandoned his half-hearted attempts to study law, and together with some actors formed a small theatre company called the Illustre-Théâtre. Changing his name to Molière (no one knows why), he performed with his troupe in a converted tennis court in Paris. They were a commercial disaster.

After a period in jail for debt, Molière formed another company and spent the next 13 years touring the provinces, honing his skills as a writer, actor and manager, and presenting traditional French farces influenced by Italian *commedia dell'arte*. By 1658 his success in the provinces had encouraged him to try once again in Paris, and on 24 October 1658, he was invited to perform in front of the young King Louis XIV at the Louvre.

Having elected to perform *Nicomède*, a tragedy by Corneille, Molière could sense half-way through the performance that it was not being well received. With a decision that would save his career and alter the course of French theatrical history, Molière stepped forward and asked to perform one of his own plays instead. The subsequent performance of *Le Docteur Amoureux*, which has since been lost, was such a success that Molière was invited to settle in Paris permanently. Over the next 15 years, he built a reputation unsurpassed in French drama.

His genius was to take the traditions of French farcical comedy, and by mixing social satire with vivid plays of character, develop it into a genre that could be as revelatory of human nature as the tragedies of his contemporaries. His best-known plays revolve around a central character (originally played by Molière himself) who personifies a folly or vice: *Le Tartuffe, Le Misanthrope, L'Avare, Le Bourgeois Gentilhomme, Le Malade Imaginaire.*

RIGHT A portrait of Molière by Pierre Mignard, in the role of Caesar in *La Mort de Pompée* by Corneille.

Incredibly industrious, Molière not only wrote and performed his own plays but was called upon to produce Comédie-Ballets for the Court. He administered the Palais-Royal during a time in which it was extensively redeveloped, pioneering many new developments in stage design and theatrical machinery. He was a great supporter of the new French writers, including the young Racine, whose first play he presented. In fact, such is his influence over the Parisian stage that the Comédie-Française is also known as La Maison de Molière – even today, the Comédie-Française produces more plays by Molière than any other playwright.

THE COMÉDIE-FRANÇAISE

It was Louis XIV who established a continuing tradition of government intervention in Parisian theatre. His interest in the theatre was not only because he liked to perform in Molière's Comédie-Ballets, but because he recognised the importance of the theatre in forging a national identity. Cardinal Richelieu had already established the Académie Française in 1630, providing a final arbiter in matters of literary taste, and now Louis XIV aimed to do just the same with the theatre.

In 1680, he amalgamated Paris' three leading theatre companies – the Hôtel de Bourgogne, the Théâtre du Marais, and Molière's old company – into one official company, called the Comédie-Française. At one stroke the oldest and most famous theatre company in Europe was born.

Despite constant upheavals, not least the replacing of the monarchy with a republic, the Comédie-Française has remained a national Institution and the great defender of France's classical tradition. With performance traditions and comic routines that have been handed down from player to player over the centuries, it still claims a direct link with *le grand siécle*. Home to some of France's greatest actors and directors, including Sarah Bernhardt, Jean-Louis Barrault, Charles Dullin and Jacques Copeau, its main theatre is the Salle Richelieu, but in the 1990s two new venues were added – the Théâtre du Vieux Colombier and the Studio theatre at the Carrousel de Louvre.

In the 20th Century, there has been one break in tradition: while formerly the oldest

ABOVE Comédie-Française in 1979 with a production of Molière's celebrated play *Le Malade Imaginaire*.

RIGHT The legendary French actress Sarah Bernhardt (1844-1923), one of the leading names of the Comédie-Française.

UN FILM DE
MARCEL CARNÉ

1ᴱᴿ ÉPOQUE
LE BOULEVARD
DU CRIME

ARLETTY . JEAN-LOUIS   BARRAULT . PIERRE BRASSEUR . PIERRE RENOIR

LES ENFANTS DU PARADI

IMAGES DE ROGER HUBERT   ᴀᵥₑc LOUIS SALOU   MARCEL HERRAND   MARIA CASARÈS   SCÉNARIO ET DIALO
DIRECTEUR DE PRODUCTION FRED ORAIN   JACQUES PRÉ

actor in the Comédie-Française ran the
company, now a resident director, appointed
to the position by the President of the
Republic, fills that role.

THE BOULEVARD THEATRE

Audiences who demanded more down-to-
earth theatrical entertainment than the
Comédie-Française had to offer found their
tastes catered for outside the city walls, in the
booths and theatres of the Paris Fairs.

Since medieval times, the Paris Fairs had
allowed provincial companies to perform near
the city, as long as they did not break the
restrictions on acting spoken text. Instead, by
mixing popular songs with mime and dance,
they presented shows that often poked fun at
the legitimate theatre. Literally meaning
'Songs of the streets', Vaudeville had its
heyday in the mid-19th Century, a period
that is celebrated in Marcel Carné's 1945 film
Les Enfants du Paradis.

The most famous home of Vaudeville was
at the boulevard du Temple, which stood
roughly on the site of the present day
boulevard Voltaire. In fact, many of the old
fairside theatres were rebuilt in permanent

ABOVE A cinema poster for
Marcel Carné's 1945
classic *Les Enfants du
Paradis*, with a screenplay
by Jacques Prévert.

ABOVE From 1899, a portrait of Georges Feydeau by Carolus Duran.

BELOW A performance at the Palais-Royal in 1989 of Feydeau's *Un Fil-à-la-Patte*.

BELOW RIGHT A poster for a film version of Feydeau's *La Dame de Chez Maxim* at a Paris cinema in 1950.

homes in the wake of Haussmann's great building work in 1862. Thus, Paris' famous boulevard theatres – the home of French commercial theatre – came into being, presenting a cocktail of melodrama, variety and farce.

The best-known exponent of the boulevard farce was Georges Feydeau. His works, considered little more than cheap entertainment in his lifetime, have become classics of the genre, even receiving definitive performances from the Comédie-Française. His farces usually revolve around respectable characters found in compromising situations, and who as a result have to resort to desperate lengths to preserve their reputations, with uproarious results. The most famous of Feydeau's repetoire of more than 60 plays include *Le Système Ribadier*, *Le Dindon*, and *La Dame de Chez Maxim*.

Today the line between the commercial and public theatres of Paris is somewhat blurred. The Comédie-Française is committed to performing contemporary plays, and many of the most successful playwrights in Paris today, such as Michel Vinaver and Yasmina Reza, present work in both sectors.

EYDEAU

PARISIAN CABARET

The 19th Century became known as the Belle Epoque, and the light-hearted sophistication of the era was epitomized by the works performed in Paris' boulevard theatres. And at the heart of the period was Parisian cabaret, in particular its most famous homes – the Folies-Bergère and the Moulin Rouge.

The Folies-Bergère was the logical evolution of French vaudeville. Presenting a typical vaudeville combination of mime and song, it opened on 1 May 1869 and soon became the fashionable place to meet and be seen. The Moulin Rouge opened 20 years later, in 1889, mounting a programme that combined dance and cabaret. After witnessing the success of the Moulin Rouge, the Folies-Bergère altered its presentation to match. Over the next 60 years, the two venues became home to Paris' most famous entertainers, including Maurice Chevalier and the legendary Mistinguett.

Jeanne-Marie Mistinguett personified the Belle Epoque. She began her career as a wise-cracking comédienne, appearing in sketches featuring typical Parisian comic characters, but she made her name as a cabaret singer and dancer. With good looks, lavish costumes and wonderful choreography, she based her act on her extraordinary personality. Throughout her career she appeared virtually exclusively in Paris, but such was her fame, and that of the venues she appeared in, that she became world-renowned.

Although her career marked the heyday of Parisian café variety, it still exists. The Moulin Rouge may be almost a parody of its former self, and the Folies-Bergère offers musicals instead of cabaret, but the spirit of outrage and glamour lives on in the café-theatres of the city. These uniquely Parisian venues offer a modern mix of alternative comedy, political satire and outrageous cabaret. Perhaps best known is Michou, where even national politicians have been seen on stage with its stunning drag queens.

THE LUMIÈRE BROTHERS

At the height of the Belle Epoque, in the basement of the Grand Café, boulevard des Capucines, a new art form was being born. It was here, on 28 December 1895, that Auguste and Louis Lumière first presented to a paying audience their Cinèmatographe, an

BELOW The undisputed queen of the Paris cabaret scene centred on the Moulin Rouge and Folies-Bergère, Mistinguett.

MISTINGUETT

MOULIN ROUGE

ABOVE Moulin Rouge, today still a spectacular neon-lit tourist attraction on the Boulevard de Clichy.

event that is acknowledged worldwide as the real birth of cinema.

Auguste and Louis Lumière had inherited their interest in the moving image from their father, who owned a factory for the development of photographic equipment and was a keen amateur photographer. Encouraged by Thomas Edison's development of the film camera, by 1894 the brothers had developed their cinèmatographe, a lightweight film camera, which was able to not only record moving images, but also develop them and project them onto a screen.

The first film they shot was called *La Sortie des Usines Lumière* (Workers Leaving the Lumière Factory). This film, like most of the others they showed at the Grand Café, was essentially a home movie – the camera merely recorded the events that were taking place around it. In fact, one of their films, *L'Arrivé d'un Train en Gare*, in which a train rushes into a station, caused such a sensation that members of the audience would duck under their seats to avoid the oncoming locomotive. (The New Wave director Jean Luc Godard would later incorporate this idea in his 1963 film *Les Carabiniers*).

Société Anonyme des Plaques et Papiers Photographiques
A. LUMIÈRE & SES FILS
CAPITAL TROIS MILLIONS
Usines à vapeur: *LYON-MONPLAISIR*
COURS GAMBETTA, RUES ST-VICTOR, ST-MAURICE ET DES TOURNELLES

NOTICE
SUR
LE CINÉMATOGRAPHE
AUGUSTE ET LOUIS LUMIÈRE

Imprimerie L. Declères et fils, place Bellecour, 16, Lyon
— 1897 —

TOP The Lumière brothers working with what was possibly the world's earliest film editing machine.

ABOVE An advertisement from 1897 for the Lumière brothers' first commercially available film projector.

Out of more than 1,400 short films made by the Lumière brothers, only one suggested the potential narrative power of the medium: *L'Arroseur Arrosé*, which is built around the visual joke of a boy standing on a gardener's hosepipe. Their interest was in the mechanical possibilities of the film camera, rather than its potential for artistic expression. Louis Lumière famously stated that he thought that his was 'an invention without a future'. It was left to others to exploit and harness the new invention.

Artistically this was done by Georges Méliès, a stage magician who recognised the possibilities for invention and fantasy in the new medium. His trademark films are *Trip to the Moon* (1902), in which a rocket lands in the eye of the 'man in the moon', and his adaptation of Jules Verne's *20,000 Leagues Under the Sea* (1907).

THE GROWTH OF THE AVANT-GARDE

The films of the Lumière brothers and Georges Méliès mark two distinct strands in French cinema – documentary realism on the one hand and visual imagination and fantasy on the other. This clash between realism and stylization is a battle that has also been played out in the French theatre throughout its history, but by the 1920s, in the wake of the carnage of the First World War, the debate had reached its height. Paris had become the avant-garde centre of the world.

ABOVE A postcard with a reproduction of a turn-of-the-century poster for the Lumière Cinématographe.

BELOW The famous still from Georges Méliès' *Voyage dans la Lune*.

EN ATTENDANT GODO

ABOVE The 1953 debut of Samuel Beckett's *Waiting for Godot* at the Théâtre de Babylone in Paris.

In the 1920s, Paris was the home of surrealism – the artistic movement that believed that the irrationality of life could be reflected by irrationality in art. Man Ray, René Clair, Luis Buñuel and Salvador Dali all produced films, and Jean Cocteau produced both films and plays that rejected external reality and replaced it with the feeling, mood and absurdity of the unconscious mind.

Modern feelings of despair and the isolation of existence also found dramatic form in the work of the mid-century existentialists Albert Camus and Jean-Paul Sartre, but while these plays espoused radical new philosophies, they presented them in a traditional dramatic structure.

In 1953, however, a new play appeared which was to combine Sartre's anguished view of the world with a dramatic style and structure which was completely new. Called *En Attendant Godot* (Waiting for Godot), it was written by Samuel Beckett, and set a style that would soon become known as the Theatre of the Absurd.

Born in Ireland, Beckett came to Paris in the wake of the literary giants that had flocked there in the 1920s and 1930s, luminaries that included James Joyce and Ernest Hemingway. His first novels, written in English, met with little success and it was not until the 1950s, by which time he had turned to writing plays in French, that his reputation was made.

En Attendant Godot was his first play, and it remains his most famous. Its presentation of two confused tramps waiting by a solitary tree for a character (Godot) who never comes has become the defining image of 20th Century drama. The characters exist only in the present and fill their time with comic routines and inane chatter – a bleakly absurd metaphor for the futility of existence.

Although *En Attendant Godot* was greeted by many with incomprehension and derision, Beckett continued to convey his vision of hopelessness and loss with plays that challenged convention and pushed back the boundaries of dramatic expression. His 1957 play *Fin de Partie* featured a blind man beside two old people in dustbins, while *Oh! les Beaux Jours* centres around a woman who is gradually buried up to her neck in sand. His 1969 play *Breath* lasted 60 seconds and had no dialogue at all.

ABOVE Samuel Beckett in his seventies – the Irish playwright died in 1989.

BELOW The French poet and actor Antonin Artaud, a seminal influence on the avant garde and pioneer of the non-verbal Theatre of Cruelty, appearing in a scene from *The Passion of Joan of Arc* in 1928.

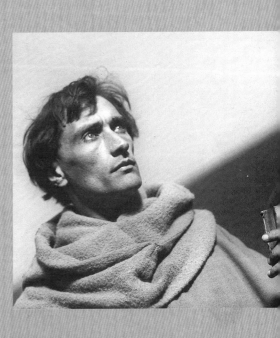

Although Beckett was certainly the most prominent, he was not the only figure in the Theatre of the Absurd. Others included Jean Genet, Arthur Adamov, and Eugene Ionesco. All the plays share themes of alienation and despair, but their use of theatricality and comedy has ensured their continuing influence and popularity although their philosophical views are considered *passé*.

The small *théâtres de poche* ('pocket theatres') that thrived in the 1950s and could afford to risk presenting Absurd plays have nearly all gone – only La Huchette survives, still presenting Ionesco's *La Cantatrice Chauve* and *La Leçon*. The majority of these small theatres were turned into cinemas in the 1960s, as French cinema underwent a revolution in form as far-reaching and internationally influential as the Theatre of the Absurd had been to French drama.

ABOVE The Théâtre de la Huchette in rue de la Huchette on the Left Bank, the last surviving *théâtre de poche*.

THE NEW WAVE

Although the ideas of the Absurdist writers could be traced back to the surrealist experiments with film in the 1920s, the coming of film-sound had pushed the cinema back towards realism. In the decade before the War, the films of Jean Renoir and Marcel Carné pioneered a style that became known as poetic realism, in which realistic scenes were integrated with powerful visual imagery. In fact, Renoir's films *La Grande Illusion* and *La Règle du Jeu* are widely considered to be

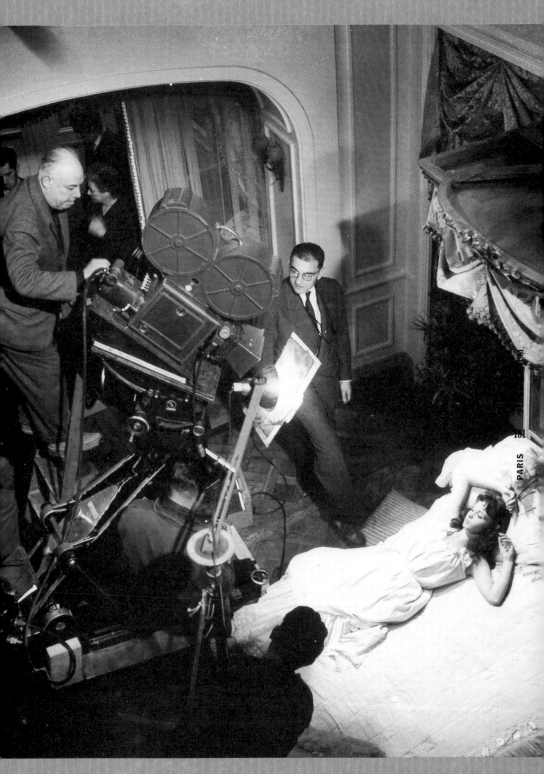

ABOVE The great film director Jean Renoir on the set of *French Can-Can* (1955) with actress Françoise Arnould.

LEFT A scene from the 1937 Renoir classic *La Grande Illusion*.

CAHIERS
DU CINÉMA

123 • REVUE MENSUELLE DE CINÉMA • SEPTEMBRE 1961 • **123**

ABOVE A 1961 edition of the influential magazine *Cahiers du Cinéma*.

LEFT A major figure in the French avant garde, the illustrator, writer and film-maker Jean Cocteau.

RIGHT A poster for the 1946 Jean Cocteau film *La Belle et la Bête* (Beauty and the Beast).

two of the greatest films ever made, but at the time of their release they made little impact. It was not until a group of young film critics championed Renoir's work that his reputation was secured.

In 1951, a new film magazine was launched, entitled *Cahiers du Cinema*. Edited by André Bazin, it counted on contributions from François Truffaut, Jean Luc Godard, Claude Chabrol and Eric Rohmer among others. Critical of the staid, predictable films that were being produced in France after the war – largely adaptations of classic novels – they praised the work of more original French film makers, such as Jacques Tati, Jean Cocteau and Renoir, all of whom were *auteurs* (or authors of their own films). Within the pages of *Cahiers du Cinéma*, Truffaut and others argued in favour of a theory known as *la politique des auteurs*, maintaining that it was only by film-makers writing, directing and producing their own films that French cinema could be revived. These contributors eventually decided to put their own ideas into practice, and the films they made gave French cinema a new relaxed and personal vision, which became known as La Nouvelle Vague, or the new wave.

The first film of La Nouvelle Vague was Claude Chabrol's *Le Beau Serge*, shown at the Cinémathèque Française in 1958. But the full impact of the new movement was not felt until the following year when Chabrol's *Les Cousins*, Godard's *A Bout de Souffle* and

JEAN MARAIS
JOSETTE DAY
dans un film de
JEAN COCTEAU

LA BELLE ET LA BÊTE

Adaptation et dialogue de JEAN COCTEAU
Décors et maquettes de CHRISTIAN BÉRARD

avec
MILA PARELY, NANE GERMON, MICHEL AUCLAIR
et MARCEL ANDRÉ
PRODUCTION ANDRÉ PAULVÉ

Truffaut's *Les 400 Coups* met with critical and commercial success.

Godard's *A Bout de Souffle* is perhaps the quintessential new wave film. Godard was given the idea for the plot by Truffaut, and the central character, Michel Poiccard, who kills a policeman and then falls for his girlfriend, is in the Truffaut mold: free, spontaneous and determined to live life to the full. However, the radical direction – the jump-cut editing and realistic use of the hand-held camera – are pure Godard. Although Truffaut became the most commercially successful member of the group, it was Godard who ruthlessly continued to experiment. His 1967 film *Week-End*, with its startling vision of social disintegration, was widely held to be a contributing factor in the violent protests that erupted on the Paris streets a year later.

BELOW Director François Truffaut behind the camera for his 1970 film *Domicile Conjugal* (Bed and Board) which he also co-scripted.

TRUFFAUT

JEANNE MOREAU

DANS UN FILM DE

FRANÇOIS TRUFFAUT

ULES
et
JIM

D'APRÈS LE ROMAN DE
HENRI-PIERRE ROCHÉ
ADAPTATION ET DIALOGUE DE
FRANÇOIS TRUFFAUT
ET JEAN GRUAULT
AVEC
OSKAR WERNER
HENRI SERRE
ET
MARIE DUBOIS
DIRECTEUR DE LA PHOTOGRAPHIE
RAOUL COUTARD

ABOVE & RIGHT A poster and still from the seminal Truffaut masterpiece *Jules et Jim* with Jeanne Moreau.

The continuing success of French film *auteurs*, such as Léos Carax, Bertrand Tavernier and Alain Resnais, has kept Paris at the cutting edge of world cinema, and its many vibrant film festivals continually introduce the work of new film-makers to an ever-interested public.

In the wake of the new wave film *auteurs*, French theatre began to wake up to the concept of the director as artist. In the 1960s, the director Roger Planchon originated the term *écriture scénique*. Meaning 'scenic writing', it placed a director's vision on a par with written text and led to Paris becoming the centre of directorial innovation in Europe. Working within their own idiosyncratic theatres, and often with an international mix of actors, these directors have created work in Paris that has toured internationally, amazing audiences and influencing theatre professionals in many other countries. Perhaps best known is the work of Ariane Mnouchkine and the Théâtre du Soleil, based at the Cartoucherie, and Peter Brook at the Bouffes du Nord.

LEFT France Brown in a production by Theatre du Soleil *La Nort des Rois*.

RIGHT Juliette Binoche and Denis Lavat in *Les Amants du Pont-Neuf*, directed by Léos Carax.

DIRECTORY

ARCHITECTURE

Arc de Triomphe
Place Charles de Gaulle
75008
01 43 80 31 31

Arène de Lutèce
Rue de Navarre 75005

Dôme Church
Hôtel National des Invalides
Avenue de Tourville 75007
01 44 42 37 67

Eiffel Tower
Champ de Mars 75007
01 44 11 23 11

Gare du Nord
Rue de Dunkerque

La Grande Arche
Paris la Défense
01 49 07 27 57

Grand Palais
Porte A
Avenue Eisenhower 75008
01 44 13 17 30

Hôtel de Ville
4 Place de l'Hôtel de Ville
75004
01 42 76 50 49

La Madeleine
Place de la Madeleine 75008
01 44 51 69 00

Notre Dame
Ile de la Cité 75001
01 42 34 56 10

Opéra de Paris Garnier
Place de l'Opéra 75009
01 40 01 18 58

Palais de Chaillot
17 Place du Trocadéro 75016

Palais de Justice
4 Boulevard du Palais 75001
01 44 32 50 00

Le Panthéon
Place du Panthéon 75005
01 43 54 34 51

Pont-Neuf
Western end of Ile-de-la-Cité,
connecting Rue Dauphine
on the Left Bank to Rue de la
Monnaie on the Right Bank

Portes St-Denis et St-Martin
Boulevards St-Denis and
St-Martin 75010

Pyramid
Cour Napoléon
Palais du Louvre 75001

Sacré-Coeur
35 Rue de Chevalier 75018
01 53 41 89 00

Sainte-Chapelle
4 Boulevard du Palais 75001
01 53 73 78 50

ART

Daniel Templon
30 Rue Beaubourg 75003
01 42 72 14 10

Galerie 1900–2000
8 Rue Bonaparte 75006
01 43 25 84 20

Lelong
13–14 Rue de Téhéran
75008
01 45 63 13 19

Musée des Arts Decoratifs
Palais du Louvre
107 Rue de Rivoli 75001
01 44 55 57 50

Musée Carnavalet
23 Rue de Sévigné 75003
01 42 72 21 13

Musée de Cluny
6 Place Paul-Painlevé 75005
01 53 73 78 00

Musée du Louvre
Palais du Louvre 75001
01 40 20 53 17

Musée de l'Orangerie
Jardin des Tuileries
Place de la Concorde 75008
01 42 97 48 16

Musée d'Orsay
1 Rue de Bellechasse 75007
01 40 49 48 14

Musée Picasso
Hôtel Salé
5 Rue de Thorigny 75003
01 42 71 25 21

Musée Rodin
77 Rue de Varenne 75007
01 47 05 01 34

Petit Palais
Avenue Winston Churchill
75008
01 42 65 12 73

Pompidou Centre
Place Georges Pompidou
Rue Beaubourg 75004
01 44 78 12 33

La Ruche
7 Passage de Dantzig 75015

FASHION

Azzedine Alaïa
7 Rue de Moussy 75004
01 40 27 85 58

Chanel
42 Avenue Montaigne
75008
01 47 20 84 45

Christian Dior
30 Avenue Montaigne
75008
01 40 73 54 44

Christian Lacroix
73 Rue du Faubourg-St-
Honoré 75008
01 42 68 79 00

Comme des Garçons
40–42 Rue Etienne-Marcel
75002
01 42 33 05 21

Gianni Versace
62 Rue du Faubourg-St-
Honoré 75008
01 47 42 88 02

Giorgio Armani
6 Place Vendôme 75001
01 42 61 55 09

Jean-Paul Gaultier
6 Rue Vivienne 75002
01 42 86 05 05

Karl Lagerfeld
19 Rue du Faubourg-St-
Honoré 75008
01 42 66 64 64

Pierre Cardin
59 Rue du Faubourg-St-
Honoré 75008
01 42 66 92 25

Thierry Mugler
49 Avenue Montaigne
75008
01 47 23 37 62

Ungaro
2 Avenue Montaigne 75008
01 53 57 00 00

Yohji Yamamoto
69 Rue des Sts-Pères 75006
01 45 48 22 56

Yves Saint Laurent
5 Avenue Marceau 75016
01 44 31 64 00

FESTIVALS

**January: La Grande Parade
de Montmartre**
Leaves Place Pigalle 75018 at
around 2pm, arriving at
Place Jules-Joffrin at 4pm
01 42 52 42 00

**End January/early Feb:
Nouvel An Chinois**
Avenues d'Ivry and de
Choisy 75013

**Good Friday: Le Chemin de
la Croix**
Procession from Place
Willette 75018 to Sacré-
Coeur
01 53 41 89 00

1 May: Fête du Travail
Procession through eastern
Paris via the Bastille 75004

**End May/early June: Les
Cinq Jours de l'Objet
Extraordinaire**
Rues du Bac, de Lille, de
Beaune, des Sts-Pères, de
l'Université and de Verneuil,
plus quai Voltaire 75005
01 42 61 31 45

Mid-June: Feux de la St-Jean
Quai St-Bernard 75005
01 43 29 21 75

**End June: Course des
Garçons et Serveuses de
Café**
4 Place de l'Hôtel de Ville
75004

**Early July: La Goutte d'Or en
Fête**
Place Léon 75019
01 53 09 99 22

**14 July: Le Quatorze Juillet
– Bastille Day**
Procession starts at 10am
from Arc de Triomphe to
Place de la Concorde; also a
firework display at the
Trocadéro in the evening,
which can be viewed from
Champ-de-Mars 75007 (the
location of the Eiffel Tower)

**14 July to 15 August: Paris,
Quartier d'Eté**
Information available from
L'Eté Parisien
01 44 83 64 40

**15 August: Fête de
l'Assomption**
Ile de la Cité 75004
01 42 34 56 10

**15 Septemper to 31
December: Festival
d'Automne**
Information available from
56 Rue de Rivoli 75001
01 53 45 17 17

October: Fête des Vendanges à Montmartre
Rue des Saules 75018
01 42 52 42 00

11 November: Armistice Day
Arc de Triomphe 75008
01 42 61 55 09

December: Crèche de Noël
Parvis de Notre-Dame 75004
01 45 80 24 52

24 December: Africolor
Théâtre Gérard-Philipe
59 Boulevard Jules-Guesde
93200 St-Denis
01 48 13 70 00

FOOD & DRINK

Au Pied de Cochon
6 Rue Coquillière 75001
01 40 13 77 00

Brasserie Flo
7 Cour des Petites-Ecuries
75010
01 47 70 13 59

Café de Flore
172 Blvd St-Germain 75006
01 45 48 55 26

Café Mouffetard
116 Rue Mouffetard 75005
01 43 31 42 50

Christian Constant
37 Rue d'Assas 75006
01 45 48 45 51

La Closerie des Lilas
171 Boulevard du
Montparnasse 75006
01 43 26 70 50

La Coupole
102 Boulevard du
Montparnasse 75014
01 43 20 14 20

Les Deux Magots
170 Blvd St-Germain 75006
01 45 48 55 25

Le Dôme
108 Boulevard du
Montparnasse 75014
01 43 35 25 81

Fauchon
26 Place de la Madeleine
75008
01 47 42 60 11

Le Grand Véfour
17 Rue de Beaujolais 75001
01 42 96 56 27

Le Jules Verne
2nd platform of Eiffel Tower
01 45 55 61 44

Lucas Carton
9 Place de la Madeleine
75008
01 42 65 22 90

Maison Berthillon
31 Rue St-Louis-en-l'lle
75004

La Maison du Chocolat
225 Rue du Faubourg-St-
Honoré 75008
01 42 27 39 44

Maison de la Truffe
19 Place de la Madeleine
75008
01 42 65 53 22

Maxim's
3 Rue Royale 75008
01 42 65 27 94

Oum El Banine
16 bis Rue Dufrenoy 75016
01 45 04 91 22

La Rotonde
105 Boulevard du
Montparnasse 75014

Tan Dinh
60 Rue de Verneuil 75007
01 45 44 04 84

La Tour d'Argent
15–17 Quai de la Tournelle
75005
01 43 54 23 31

MUSIC

Casino de Paris
16 Rue de Clichy 75009
01 49 95 22 22

La Cigale
120 Boulevard Rochechouart
75018
01 49 25 89 99

Cité de la Musique
Parc de La Villette
221 Avenue Jean-Jaurès
75019
01 44 84 45 00

Club St-Germain
13 Rue St-Benoît 75006
01 45 48 81 84

New Opus Café
167 Quai de Valmy 75010
01 40 34 70 00

Olympia
28 Boulevard des Capucines
75009
01 47 42 25 49

Opéra Comique
5 Rue Favart 75002
01 42 44 45 46

Opéra de Paris Bastille
120 Rue de Lyon 75012
01 40 01 17 89

Salle Pleyel
252 Rue du Faubourg-St-
Honoré 75008
01 45 61 53 00

Théâtre des Champs-Élysées
15 Avenue Montaigne 75008
01 49 52 50 50

Théâtre du Châtelet
2 Rue Edouard-Colonne
75001
01 40 28 28 40

Théâtre de la Ville
2 Place du Châtelet 75001
01 42 74 22 77

SPORTS

Aquaboulevard
(Massive aquatic fun park)
4 Rue Louis-Armand 75015
01 40 60 10 00

Fédération Française de Football
60 bis Avenue d'Iéna 75016
01 44 31 73 00

Fédération Française du Golf
69 Avenue Victor-Hugo
75016
01 44 17 63 00

Fédération Française de Pétanque et Jeux Provençales
(For information on pétanque and other games)
9 Rue Duperré 75009
01 48 74 61 63

Fédération Française de Sport Automobile
136 Rue de Longchamp
75016
01 44 30 24 00

Fédération des Sociétés des Courses de France
(For information on horse-racing venues and events)
22 Rue de Penthièvre 75008
01 42 25 96 71

Hippodrome d'Auteuil
(Steeplechasing venue)
Bois de Boulogne 75016
01 45 20 15 98

Hippodrome de Longchamp
(Flat-racing venue)
Bois de Boulogne 75016
01 44 30 75 00

Hippodrome de Vincennes
(Trotting races venue)
2 Route de la Ferme 75012
01 49 77 17 17

Ligue Parisienne de Football
5 Place de Valois 75001
01 42 61 56 47

Palais Omnisports de Paris-Bercy (Sports hall)
8 Boulevard de Bercy 75012
01 40 02 61 67

Parc des Princes
(Sports stadium)
24 Rue du Commandant-Guilbaud 75016
01 42 88 02 76

Stade Roland Garros
(Host to the French Open tennis tournament)
2 Avenue Gordon-Bennett
75016
01 47 43 48 00

STAGE & FILM

Atelier
Place Charles Dullin 75018
01 46 06 49 24

Café de la Gare
41 Rue du Temple 75004
01 42 78 52 51

Comédie des Champs-Elysées
15 Avenue Montaigne 75008
01 53 23 99 19

Comédie-Française
2 Rue de Richelieu 75001
01 40 15 00 15

Folies-Bergères
32 Rue Richer 75009
01 44 79 98 98

Hébertot
78 bis Boulevard des Batignolles 75017
01 43 87 23 23

Huchette
23 Rue de la Huchette
75005
01 43 26 38 99

Moulin Rouge
82 Boulevard de Clichy
75018
01 46 06 00 19

Odéon Théâtre de l'Europe
(aka Théâtre National de l'Odéon)
Place de l'Odéon 75006
01 44 41 36 36

Palais-Royal
38 Rue Montpensier 75001
01 42 97 59 81

Shakespeare Garden
(Open-air theatre)
Bois de Boulogne 75016
01 42 76 55 06

Théâtre National de Chaillot
Place du Trocadéro 75016
01 47 27 81 15

Théâtre National de la Colline
15 Rue Malte-Brun 75020
01 44 62 52 52

Théâtre du Soleil
Cartoucherie
Route du Champ-des-Manoeuvres 75012
01 43 74 24 08

PICTURE CREDITS

The publishers wish to thank the following individuals and organizations for their kind permission to reproduce the photographs in this book. Every effort has been made to credit the artists, photographers and organizations whose work has been included and we apologize for any unintentional omissions.